Cambridge Elements

Elements in Music Since 1945
edited by
Mervyn Cooke
University of Nottingham

ELLIOTT CARTER'S STRING QUARTET NO. 1

Myths, Narratives, and Cold War Cultural Diplomacy

Laura Emmery
Emory University

Shaftesbury Road, Cambridge CB2 8EA, United Kingdom

One Liberty Plaza, 20th Floor, New York, NY 10006, USA

477 Williamstown Road, Port Melbourne, VIC 3207, Australia

314–321, 3rd Floor, Plot 3, Splendor Forum, Jasola District Centre, New Delhi – 110025, India

103 Penang Road, #05–06/07, Visioncrest Commercial, Singapore 238467

Cambridge University Press is part of Cambridge University Press & Assessment, a department of the University of Cambridge.

We share the University's mission to contribute to society through the pursuit of education, learning and research at the highest international levels of excellence.

www.cambridge.org
Information on this title: www.cambridge.org/9781009537131

DOI: 10.1017/9781009537124

First published 2024

A catalogue record for this publication is available from the British Library

ISBN 978-1-009-53713-1 Hardback
ISBN 978-1-009-53714-8 Paperback
ISSN 2632-7791 (online)
ISSN 2632-7783 (print)

Elliott Carter's String Quartet No. 1

Myths, Narratives, and Cold War Cultural Diplomacy

Elements in Music Since 1945

DOI: 10.1017/9781009537124
First published online: December 2024

Laura Emmery
Emory University

Author for correspondence: Laura Emmery, laura.emmery@emory.edu

Abstract: This Element offers a critical analysis of the history of Elliott Carter's String Quartet No. 1 and the composer's rise to public acclaim, not through the study of the work itself but through intriguing and captivating narratives that surround this quartet and their socio-cultural-political context, which led Carter to become one of the most dominant voices in the post-1945 American music scene. Carter's road to success was meticulously paved by powerful institutions and individuals, including critics, scholars, festival and radio programming directors, and the US government, for whom, in the context of the Cold War, Carter was chosen to represent an exemplary American triumphant story. The author argues that it is not the quartet itself that contributed to Carter's reception and legacy, but the inextricable narratives that we associate with this work.

This Element also has a video abstract: Cambridge.org/
EM45_Emmery_abstract

Keywords: Elliott Carter, String Quartet No. 1, twentieth-century string quartet, American modernism, Cold War cultural diplomacy, music and politics, music and narrative, intertextuality

ISBNs: 9781009537131 (HB), 9781009537148 (PB), 9781009537124 (OC)
ISSNs: 2632-7791 (online), 2632-7783 (print)

Contents

Introduction: History and Reception of Elliott Carter's String Quartet No. 1

Elliott Carter (1908–2012) played a pivotal role in defining American musical modernism after the Second World War. Sponsored by the Congress for Cultural Freedom (CCF), whose mission was to organize cultural events that promoted American artists and intellectuals, Carter became one of the most prominent American voices during the Cold War period. He would receive the Pulitzer Prize for Music twice – in 1960 for his String Quartet No. 2, and in 1973 for String Quartet No. 3. But it was his String Quartet No. 1 (1950–51) that marked a turning point in the development of his new musical language and expression and, as David Schiff – Carter's former student at Juilliard – notes, "put Carter on the musical map."[1]

Scholars have singled out Carter's five string quartets as his most essential and recognized works. Schiff, for instance, refers to them as "the spinal column of his body of work."[2] Among them, String Quartet No. 1 has been the most celebrated, performed, recorded, and analyzed. It debuted Carter's novel ideas that he was developing at the time, including the individualization of instruments, superimposition of thematic material, use of complex polyrhythms, tempo modulations, chordal sonorities as a means of unifying the work, intricate textures, and novel forms.[3] Jonathan Bernard, while discussing the beginnings of Carter's "mature" works (with compositions such as the Cello Sonata [1948], the Woodwind Quintet [1948], *Eight Etudes and a Fantasy* [1949–50], and *Eight Pieces for Four Timpani* [1949]), noted that with String Quartet No. 1, "the first breakthrough was still to come."[4] Bernard further observes that the Quartet, which in 1953 was submitted anonymously to a string quartet competition in Liège, Belgium, won first prize and thereafter received wide exposure both in Europe and the United States, consequently "establish[ing] Carter's reputation for good."[5] Schiff describes String Quartet No. 1 as "the grandest of the quartets in conception, the one that stands closest, for all the innovations of its syntax, to Beethovenian models,"[6] declaring the Quartet and Carter worthy of such recognition and attention.

In short, the reputation of Carter's String Quartet No. 1 has reached mythical proportions, an image that was carefully crafted by scholars, the powerful institutions that supported him, and Carter himself. At the time the Quartet was being glorified and cementing Carter's placement "on the musical map,"

---

[1] Schiff, *The Music of Elliott Carter*, 53.   [2] Schiff, *The Music of Elliott Carter*, 53.

[3] Emmery, *Compositional Process in Elliott Carter's String Quartets: A Study in Sketches*, 3.

[4] Bernard, "The String Quartets of Elliott Carter," 239.

[5] Bernard, "The String Quartets of Elliott Carter," 239.

[6] Schiff, *The Music of Elliott Carter*, 53–55.

virtually no one had heard this work. Although Virgil Thomson eventually wrote a positive review of the work, the premiere by the Walden Quartet of the University of Illinois on February 27, 1953,[7] received a lukewarm reception, which Carter mentioned in his early drafts of the program notes of the quartet:

> I invited one excellent quartet to our apartment in N.Y. when I had completed the work to try and read it over and they couldn't – and it's not surprising because the notation which I needed to put down my ideas, although much reduced, [...] is extremely curious and unusual. However, I sent it to one group, and Walden Quartet, who made this record and to whom I later dedicated this work, who surprised me greatly after a six month's silence by writing that they had been learning the quartet and were going to play it at a [subscription] concert at Columbia University in February 1953. It was rather lukewarmly received but got very good reviews in the press. Then I sent the work to a prize contest in Liege, Belgium. Later the work had another performance at an ISCM concert given by the Waldens in New York at which it was very successful and received a glowing review from Virgil Thomson.[8]

Following the premiere, Carter submitted the quartet to a small and unknown string quartet competition in Liège, Belgium, the same year, where it was awarded first prize before being disqualified for having had a prior public performance. String Quartet No. 1 did not receive wider recognition until a year later, in 1954 when it was performed at the Rome Festival, where it also received mixed reviews,[9] and then two years later, in 1956, when it was recorded by the Walden Quartet.

Thus, a question arises: How did String Quartet No. 1 contribute to Carter's meteoric rise and notoriety so early on? After all, it is a piece that only a small, exclusive audience in New York City had heard (until the Rome performance and subsequentially the first available recording in 1956), that only one ensemble could play at the time (and whose premiere was not well received), and that had won a rather insignificant award before it was disqualified from that competition.

---

[7] String Quartet No. 1 was premiered on February 26, 1953, at the McMillan Theater, Columbia University (New York City) by the Walden Quartet of the University of Illinois with Homer Schmitt (violin 1), Bernard Goodman (violin 2), John Garvey (viola), and Robert Swenson (cello).

[8] The Elliott Carter Collection, String Quartet No. 1, "Einführungstext" [Introduction], Paul Sacher Stiftung, Basel, Switzerland.

[9] In *Elliott Carter: A Centennial Portrait in Letters and Documents* (101n42), Felix Meyer and Anne C. Shreffler note that one critic found the quartet "impenetrable" (Fedele d'Amico, "Current Chronicle"), while Reginald Smith Brindle wrote that the quartet "showed exceptionally virile writing, but a fantasy so uncontrolled that it abandoned musical coherence" ("Notes from Abroad"), and that an Austrian critic, Helmuth A. Fiechtner, did not mention the piece at all in his review of the concert ("Tonkunst und Debatten beim Römischen Musikkongreß").

Unquestionably, Carter's String Quartet No. 1 is a seminal work in the composer's oeuvre, which introduced many novel ideas that would define his new musical style and expression. That is, the ideas Carter had been developing since 1944 found their fullest expression in his First Quartet. For instance, Carter remarks that String Quartet No. 1 marked his "most extreme adventure" into "metric modulation" – a seamless shift from one tempo into another, which becomes integrated with surface rhythms.[10] The Quartet also features a complex superimposition and juxtaposition of multiple textures of differing speeds, rhythms, and characters; an individualization of instruments; a harmonic language based on all-interval tetrachords; and a formal structure that features four movements that flow into one another, but with the stream of music being broken twice by dramatic pauses, pauses that do not coincide with the beginnings or endings of the movements.

Out of nearly 180 compositions in Carter's oeuvre, String Quartet No. 1 is most often analyzed – from its harmonic, rhythmic, metric, formal, and textural structure to its compositional process, literary influences, and the work's reception[11] – as well as performed and recorded.[12] As a Carter scholar myself, I was drawn to these (complex) musical features and I have certainly contributed to its scholarship. In this Element, I offer a new analysis of Carter's String Quartet No. 1: not by analyzing the piece itself, but by examining the intriguing and captivating narratives that helped propel Carter's First Quartet to its success, including the socio-cultural-political context in which these narratives were born and continued to live, and the powerful institutions and individuals who supported Carter's rise to becoming one of the most dominant American composers.

Carter supplies some of the answers for his early success in his "The General History of My String Quartet" document preserved at the Paul Sacher Stiftung (Basel, Switzerland). Despite the work's rather tepid premiere, the 1953 performance

---

[10] Emmery, *Compositional Process in Elliott Carter's String Quartets*, 7.

[11] For instance, see Bernard, "Problems of Pitch Structure in Elliott Carter's First and Second String Quartets"; Emmery, "Evolution and Process in Elliott Carter's String Quartets," "In Disguise: Musical Borrowings in Elliott Carter's Early String Quartets," "Elliott Carter's First String Quartet: In Search of Proustian Time," and *Compositional Process in Elliott Carter's String Quartets*; Lochhead, "On the 'Framing' Music of Elliott Carter's First String Quartet"; Mailman, "Temporal Dynamic Form in Music: Atonal, Tonal, and Other"; A. Mead, "Time Management: Rhythm as a Formal Determinant in Certain Works of Elliott Carter"; Meyer and Shreffler, *Elliott Carter: A Centennial Portrait in Letters and Documents*; Noubel, *Elliott Carter ou le temps fertile*; Rao, "*Allegro scorrevole* in Carter's First String Quartet: Crawford and the Ultramodern Inheritance"; Schiff, *The Music of Elliott Carter*; Schmidt, "'I Try to Write Music That Will Appeal to an Intelligent Listener's Ear.' On Elliott Carter's String Quartets"; Taruskin, *The Oxford History of Western Music*, vol. 5: The Late Twentieth Century; Wierzbicki, *Elliott Carter*.

[12] String Quartet No. 1 has been recorded by the Walden Quartet of the University of Illinois (1956); the Composer's Quartet (1970); the Arditti String Quartet (1988); the Juilliard String Quartet (1991; 2014); and the Pacifica Quartet (2008).

received "a glowing review" from Virgil Thomson, who was the most significant music critic in the United States at the time. Carol Oja, for instance, writes that Thomson – who had worked as a critic since the early 1920s, first for the *Boston Evening Transcript, Vanity Fair,* and *Modern Music* before moving to the *New York Herald Tribune,* a position he held from 1940 through 1954 – became "one of the most prominent opinion shapers of the second and third quarters of the twentieth century."[13] In his lectures and interviews dating from this period, Carter also remarked that the composers themselves had stepped into the role of critics and Carter himself worked with Thomson as a critic for the *New York Herald Tribune* for several years. Carter further explains that in order to secure the programming of new music at concerts, these "composers-critics" would generally not go to concerts unless contemporary music was played, jokingly admitting that this practice was "a kind of blackmail that resulted in many performances of contemporary music."[14] Carter also noted that in New York, Thomson refused to go to concerts that did not program music by American composers, affirming that it greatly helped all composers, especially since he would not review concerts unless the music of "important American composers" was played."[15] Lightheartedly, Carter concludes that this behavior "jacked up the field greatly," even if Thomson did not always give "good reviews."[16]

Unsurprisingly, Carter's colleague and friend Thomson wrote a favorable review of the premiere of String Quartet No. 1, dubbing it "A Powerful Work": "The piece is complex of texture, delicious in sound, richly expressive, and in every way grand. Its specific charm is the way in which it sounds less like a classical string quartet than like four intricately integrated solos all going on at the same time [. . .] It is an original and powerful piece, and the audience loved it."[17]

Following Thomson's glowing review and the announcement that the Quartet had won a string quartet competition in Liège, Belgium, the work was performed on April 11, 1954 by the Parrenin Quartet at the Music in the Twentieth Century festival in Rome, Italy, organized by Nicolas Nabokov, Carter's close friend, and sponsored by the Congress for Cultural Freedom, in which Nabokov served as Secretary General (Figure 1).[18] This crucial performance, attended by Luigi Dallapiccola, Goffredo Petrassi, Roman Vlad, and William Glock (who shortly after became the head of music at the BBC), as Schiff notes, resulted in "immediately establish[ing] Carter's European

---

[13] Oja, *Making Music Modern: New York in the 1920s,* 281.
[14] Emmery, *Elliott Carter Speaks: Unpublished Lectures,* 33.
[15] Emmery, *Elliott Carter Speaks,* 33.
[16] Emmery, *Elliott Carter Speaks,* 33.
[17] Thomson, "A Powerful Work," in *Music Chronicles, 1940–1954,* 370.
[18] See Schiff, *The Music of Elliott Carter,* 55.

Figure 1 Parrenin Quartet performs Elliott Carter's String Quartet No. 1 at the Rome Festival in April 1954. Photo by Elio Soro, Agenzia fotografica (Paul Sacher Stiftung, Basel. Used with permission).

reputation."[19] Other commendations for Carter's String Quartet No. 1 began to pour in from across the United States and abroad. Michael Steinberg wrote an adulation of the performance in Rome in his 1954 review for the *New York Times*: "Not in years has such an addition to quartet literature been made, and perhaps one must reach back as far as the Fourth Quartet of Béla Bartók to find its peer."[20]

William Glock, Carter's close friend, whom Carter described as "an early champion of the work," in June 1954 wrote the following review in *Encounter*, a British-American journal Taruskin described as the "Congress's English-language organ":[21]

> Coming directly afterwards in the same program, Schönberg's *Piano Suite*, Op. 25, seemed hardly more difficult than Kuhlau or Clementi. Yet I did not feel that Carter had introduced difficulties for their own sake; rather that he was bursting with novel ideas and was determined to give them full-grown treatment . . . In its texture the Quartet is more complex than any other I have ever heard. In the first

---

[19] Schiff, *The Music of Elliott Carter*, 55.

[20] Steinberg, "Rome Fete Hears 3 Chamber Works," 40. The review is also featured on the liner notes for the 1956 Walden recording of Carter's String Quartet No. 1 for Columbia Records, accessible via *Internet Archive*, "Full text of 'String Quartet,'" https://archive.org/stream/lp_string-quartet_elliott-carter-the-walden-string-quartet/lp_string-quartet_elliott-carter-the-walden-string-quartet_djvu.txt.

[21] Taruskin, *The Oxford History of Western Music*, vol. 5, ch. 7, § Reception.

movement especially the four instruments always have contrasting rhythms and outlines; and although the rhythmic ensemble becomes somewhat simpler as the work proceeds, there are no passages that could be described as points of rest . . . Yet it would be quite wrong to suggest that Carter does nothing more than subject us to forty-five minutes of admirable hell. On the contrary, there are many moments of striking imagination.[22]

Desmond Shawe-Taylor in his 1954 review for the *The New Statesman & Nation* expounds on Carter's impressive undertaking with this work:

An immense and formidable Quartet by Elliott Carter which I found continuously absorbing and impressive – the unmistakably decisive utterance of a new voice [. . .] each of the players appears to be improvising to his heart's content, regardless of his neighbor, yet is also mysteriously contributing to the massive onward drive and logic of the whole movement . . . he has something to say which is urgent and very much his own.[23]

On January 5, 1956, following a performance by the California String Quartet, Alfred Frankenstein, in the *San Francisco Chronicle*, remarked on Carter's already recognizable unique expression, while also placing Carter's work among the established "greats" of this period – Bartók and Schoenberg: "It is an extremely long work – 45 minutes – but its loftiness, grandeur, and power justify its size. That Carter has lived in the age of Bartók and Schönberg is obvious but he has absorbed his indebtedness into an extremely important style of his own, one that is especially remarkable for its rhythmic complexities and the freedom of its part-writing."[24]

In addition to the advantageously positive reviews, it was likely Virgil Thomson who secured the recording of Carter's String Quartet No. 1 with Columbia Records. That is, Thomson served as the chairman of the committee of American composers, who reached out to Columbia and proposed the recording of music by American composers under the Modern American Music Series. The committee, also comprising Aaron Copland, Henry Cowell, and William Schuman, would select the genres, composers, works, and specific performers that they wanted to record, which included Walden Quartet's 1956 recording of Carter's String Quartet No. 1.[25] The liner notes to the Walden Quartet performance on Columbia Records explain how the recording came about:

The present project for recording modern American music comes out of a conversation between an American composer and an official of Columbia

---

[22] Liner notes for the 1956 Walden recording.
[23] Liner notes for the 1956 Walden recording.
[24] Frankenstein, "California String Quartet Offers Concert Eloquence," 25. The review is also featured on the liner notes for the 1956 Walden recording.
[25] See Kerman, "American Music: The Columbia Series," for the history of the formation of the music series, its role, and impact.

Records, in which the composer alleged that the gramophone companies were neglecting their duty. "American music gets published and performed all over the world nowadays, but the recording companies pretend it doesn't exist. And every year the backlog of unrecorded American music gets vaster." That is what the composer said to the business man.

The business man replied to the composer, "I'll change all that if you will show me how to do it."

So together they made out the following plan. Columbia will record a minimum, in this series, of six "Lp" [sic] Records (12 sides) a year of modern American music, the works to be chosen by a committee of American composers serving without pay. These works will be recorded in each case by artists of the composer's choice working under his immediate direction or supervision. The performance will therefore be authentic as well as first-class. And the works will represent, in the judgment of the composers' committee, American music at its most distinguished and beautiful.

The committee has sought to avoid the duplication of works already available to the public in recorded form or announced for early release by other companies. Music by committee members will be included in the series in selections made by the other members of the committee. Chamber music has been chosen as the present repertory of the project, because that is the field of American music that has hitherto received the least attention from recording companies.

. . .

THE COMMITTEE
VIRGIL THOMSON, *Chairman*

AARON COPLAND
Chairman of the Faculty
Berkshire Music Center

HENRY COWELL
Professor of Composition
Peabody Institute of Music
Baltimore, Md.

GODDARD LIEBERSON
Executive Vice-President
Columbia Records

WILLIAM SCHUMAN
President
Juilliard School of Music[26]

Now we understand better how Carter's inner circle paved his road to success – the composers, who served as critics and were on the programming boards and

---

[26] The liner notes for the 1956 Walden Recording of Carter's String Quartet No. 1 for Columbia Records.

committees for festivals and recording contracts, all worked together to promote their own music, or as Carter called it, "jacking up the field." Even though Schiff remarks that Carter's path "certainly did not fit the usual model of musical development,"[27] it is evident that with his connections his path and success could not have been any more assured: on a recommendation by Charles Ives, Carter studied composition at Harvard with Walter Piston, which he followed with studies with Nadia Boulanger in Paris for three years (1932–35). Soon after, he would receive two Guggenheim and the American Academy in Rome fellowships, become an elected member of the Institute of Arts and Letters, serve as a critic for the *New York Herald Tribune*, and hold an active role in the International Society for Contemporary Music, the League of Composers, and the American Composers Alliance.

Thus, Carter himself contributed the mythical narratives, seeking to distance himself from his prewar "American" music and establish his new ideas in the context of the postwar modernist impulse, actively impacting the meteoric success of his String Quartet No. 1. In his conversation with Allen Edwards, Carter candidly revealed his attitude toward his need to develop new ideas and his lack of concern for the reception of the quartet:

> I worked up to one crucial experience, my First Quartet, written around 1950, in which I decided for once to write a work very interesting to myself, and to say to hell with the public and with the performers too. I wanted to write a work that carried out completely the various ideas I had at that time about the form of music, about texture and harmony – about everything.[28]

Yet, archival documents reveal that while Carter was composing the Quartet, he was very much concerned with what the critics, the audiences, and the performers would think of his new ideas – he worried the quartet would never get performed because of its technical difficulties, the performers "grumble[d] about" performing this music, and that the piece would be "too much for most audiences to take."[29] It would take him quite some time and several drafts of the program notes to reach the self-assured infamous line, "to hell with the public and with the performers too." While in his latest book on Carter, Schiff

---

[27] Schiff, *Carter*, 43.

[28] Edwards, *Flawed Words and Stubborn Sounds: A Conversation with Elliott Carter*, 35.

[29] See Emmery, "Elliott Carter's First String Quartet: In Search of Proustian Time," 2–4; *Compositional Process in Elliott Carter's String Quartets*, 8–9. In the earlier drafts of the program notes, Carter notes: "While writing this work, I often thought that it would never be played and if it were played it would be too much for most audiences to take." In another draft, he reiterates these concerns by writing, "While writing this st[ring]q[uartet], it occurred frequently to me that the Quartet might never be played because of its technical difficulty and that even if played it might be almost too much to expect any audience, no matter how familiar with contemporary music, to accept."

retrospectively acknowledges that over time "Carter's story ... mixed fact and mythology in a seductive way that seems increasingly problematic, though not necessarily deceitful,"[30] early Carter scholars and critics, nonetheless, greatly contributed to the formation of the mythical narrative surrounding String Quartet No. 1. As Richard Taruskin writes, "David Schiff's frankly hagiographic account" paints the undisguised picture of Carter's String Quartet No. 1 as "uncompromising and visionary."[31] Taruskin continues with a crucial observation, recognizing that Schiff's use of words like "uncompromising" "monastic seclusion," or "conversion" to describe this work carried "social and political as well as religious connotations in the context of the Cold war."[32]

In the following sections, I will closely scrutinize the narratives surrounding String Quartet No. 1 that greatly contributed to Carter's incredible success. I argue that it was not necessarily the work itself, which was neither well known nor understood at the time, and whose early performances had received lukewarm and mixed reviews, but rather the compelling narratives developed by the powerful critics, scholars, institutions, and Carter himself that ensured his triumph. Particularly, I will focus on the accounts of the "desert myth," intertextuality and extramusical associations, musical borrowings and homages, the Liège competition, and the Cold War political ideals of individualism and freedom to demystify Carter's spectacular and not entirely surprising rise to the top.

1 The Desert Myth Narrative

Elliott Carter's "Desert Myth" narrative is all too familiar: after receiving a Guggenheim Fellowship in 1950 (his second), Carter decided to leave his "usual New York activities to seek the undisturbed quiet," where he could work out his new musical experiences and processes.[33] As Carter jots down in an unpublished note, he had been waiting for just such an opportunity "to give form to a number of novel ideas that [he] had been thinking about over the past previous years, and work out bit by bit a composition of suitable character."[34] Carter found the "undisturbed quiet" in the desert near Tucson, Arizona, where he settled down to an "arduous year's work building up a whole world of musical thinking and feeling," in which every detail, practically, was a step

---

[30] Schiff, *The Music of Elliott Carter*, 59.
[31] Taruskin, *The Oxford History of Western Music*, vol. 5, 280.
[32] Taruskin, *The Oxford History of Western Music*, vol. 5, 280.
[33] Schiff, *The Music of Elliott Carter*, 54.
[34] Elliott Carter Collection, String Quartet No. 1, Text manuscripts, "Einführungstext" (Paul Sacher Stiftung, Basel).

into an "unexplored and novel realm."[35] The piece that emerged from Carter's year in the desert was his seminal String Quartet No. 1.

In his 2018 article, Sudip Bose effectively illustrates the jarring dissonance of Carter's striking decision to withdraw for a year into the Sonoran Desert and the outcome of that decision:

> So in 1950, the Manhattan-born, Harvard-educated, Paris-trained composer took a dramatic step: along with his wife and young son, Carter left New York and ended up spending more than a year in Arizona, in the vast and remote lower Sonoran Desert. There, amid the silent and austere wilderness of cacti and mesquite, of quail, snakes, horned toads, and lizards, Carter experienced something akin to a religious conversion. He wrote just one piece of music during the autumn and winter of 1950 and the spring of 1951: his String Quartet No. 1, a difficult piece unlike anything he had composed before, boldly atonal, and governed by a novel sense of rhythm, meter, and time.[36]

Carter's own desert narrative contributed to the "mythology" surrounding String Quartet No. 1, a story that Carter scholars turned into religious imagery, as Taruskin notes.[37] For instance, Schiff writes that Carter's friends "refer to this time in the desert" as his "monastic seclusion" and a "conversion," after which a "new composer emerged."[38] However, Carter's experience in the desert was neither "monastic" nor "hermetic."[39] For one, Carter was with his family during his stay in the Sonoran Desert, in the vicinity of Tucson, a city that was rapidly growing in the 1950s. Further, he met and conversed with other people daily, such as Joseph Wood Krutch (a naturalist, who was writing *The Desert Year* at the time). Notably, Carter also took breaks from his "seclusion" to explore the Arizona landscape, attended various lectures and events, and even visited Conlon Nancarrow in Mexico City, Mexico.[40] Yet, the carefully crafted desert narrative of the monastic seclusion (which incorrectly implies that Carter's wife and son were not with him) and the ensuing "conversion" created a compelling story that gave Carter – and the genesis of his String Quartet No. 1 – a certain depth and validation: a composer, who was willing to abandon New York City, the center of modernism (vividly described in Oja's seminal book, *Making*

---

[35] Elliott Carter Collection, String Quartet No. 1, Text manuscripts, "Einführungstext" (Paul Sacher Stiftung, Basel). For a published version of the note, see Schiff, *The Music of Elliott Carter*, 54.

[36] Bose, "A Year in the Desert: Elliott Carter and His Revolutionary First String Quartet."

[37] Taruskin, *The Oxford History of Western Music*, vol. 5, 280. Taruskin cites Schiff, *The Music of Elliott Carter*, 54–55.

[38] Schiff, *The Music of Elliott Carter*, 55.

[39] See Taruskin, *The Oxford History of Western Music*, vol. 5, 280.

[40] See Schiff, *The Music of Elliott Carter*, 100.

Music Modern), for a secluded desert to dedicate himself entirely to his craft, required to be taken seriously.

Perhaps, akin to the Biblical Exodus – a forty-year-long journey of Israelites through the desert in a flight from bondage in Egypt – Carter, too, at the age of forty-two embarked on a self-discovery journey through the desert, fleeing the bondage of his noisy and routine life in New York City and his prewar traditional (neoclassical) compositional style. But why specifically the desert imagery? In his book, *The Sacred Desert: Religion, Literature, Art, and Culture*, David Jasper notes that the desert "tests the people up to and beyond their limits."[41] It is a place where people go to find "new beginnings."[42] Thus, when David Klemm poses the question, "Why do they leave the shelter of all things familiar?," he concludes that "to wander in the desert is a metaphor for the human situation, once our eyes are opened to the truth that all philosophical theology reveals."[43] Scrutinizing this religious connotation further by borrowing the terminology from Edward W. Said, Jasper likens the Biblical Exodus to Kant's "exodus" into the "freedom of reason," which is associated with a journey across the desert. The "desert," of course, is understood as a space both interior and exterior: "The 'desert' refers to a complex locus of experience and reflection; it is simultaneously an interior space of the mind; an exterior place where pilgrims, adventurers, and travelers can visit and dwell; and an intertextual space produced by cross-references among cultural creations dealing with the desert as archetype or icon of the imagination."[44]

Because of its subjective and multifaceted connotations, the desert has fascinated artists, poets, and composers for centuries.[45] While Jasper observes

---

[41] Jasper, *The Sacred Desert: Religion, Literature, Art, and Culture*, 16.

[42] Jasper, *The Sacred Desert*, 4. Although Carter was not a particularly religious man and his experience and quest for self-discovery in the desert were not religious in a theological sense, Jasper notes that for many, the desert represents a new place from which "theological articulation can be found and recovered" (4). As an example, he points to Schoenberg's musical, verbal, and dramatic quest for his "inconceivable God" in his great, yet unfinished, "desert" opera *Moses and Aaron*, which is set to the *Book of Exodus*, the second book of the Bible, or to Heidegger in his reflections on the origin of the work of art, thus "both wanderers in the intermediary space between presence and absence that alone bears the key to that pure presence that the theologian Tom Altizer names the 'self-embodiment of God'" (4).

[43] Klemm, "Foreword" in *The Sacred Desert: Religion, Literature, Art, and Culture*, xi. Klemm opens the text with a rhetorical question, "Who wanders in the desert?," noting that in this book, the author converses with the "poets, prophets, mystics, madmen, nomads, explorers, outlaws, warriors, seekers, thinkers, theologians, visionaries, and artists of the desert – dreamers all" to find out what they are doing in the desert ("They are passing beyond the familiar world of stable meanings and predictable events into a domain of openness and insecurity"), and why they are there.

[44] Klemm, "Foreword," xii.

[45] As one anonymous reviewer aptly remarks, Carter's image of an American composer who is associated with the desert is far from unique; this connotation is reflected in the title of Walter Zimmermann's 1976 book, *Desert Plants: Conversations with 23 American Musicians*. Further,

that in a poet's mythic imagination, the desert becomes the Waste Land,[46] bringing to mind T. S. Eliot's physical description of the desert landscape but also a metaphorical image of death, decay, brokenness, and loss in his 1922 poem, *The Waste Land*, Aidan Tynan effectively describes the artists' attraction toward the desert, with all its dichotomies and oppositions: "We can grasp [the desert] as a natural wilderness or as a barren wasteland, as an ecology sometimes unusually rich in life and surprisingly fragile, as an idea of geographical extremity or alterity, as a sacred or accursed site, as a metaphor for nullity, as a subjective or existential terrain, or as an object of sheer aesthetic exultation."[47]

For Carter, it is precisely this "magical kingdom" of the desert that left an indelible mark on his journey of self-discovery – both from the experience of seclusion and from the musical inspiration he had drawn from the desert ecology. It also mirrors the experience and fascination his close friend, Edgard Varèse, described during his two-year exploration of the deserts of Santa Fe, New Mexico, in 1936–37 while working on *Espace*, an elaborate project that he would eventually abandon but use its sketches to compose *Déserts* (1950–54).[48] For Varèse, the desert existed not only in nature but also in one's mind or space,[49] as he explained:

> For me "deserts" is a highly evocative word. It suggests space, solitude, detachment. To me it means not only deserts of sand, sea, mountains and snow, of outer space, of deserted city streets, not only those stripped aspects of nature that suggest bareness and aloofness but also the remote inner space of the mind no telescope can reach, a world of mystery and essential loneliness.[50]

In other letters, Varèse expounds, "I have chosen deserts because I feel them and love them, and because in the United States this subject offers unlimited possibility of images which are the very essence of a poetry and magic."[51] Even twenty years later, in his program notes for String Quartet No. 1, Carter vividly remembers his discussions with Joseph Krutch about the ecology of the desert, and also evokes Thomas Mann's novel *The*

---

the metaphorical image of the "frontier" of the American West and American composers' search of their identity is the theme of Beth Levy's book, *Frontier Figures: American Music and the Mythology of the American West*. I would like to thank the reviewer for this insightful comment and for pointing me to these sources.

[46] Jasper, *The Sacred Desert*, 71.

[47] Tynan, *The Desert in Modern Literature and Philosophy: Wasteland Aesthetics*, 1.

[48] See Chou wen-Chung, "Varèse: A Sketch of the Man and His Music," 166.

[49] Gillespie, "Chou Wen-Chung on Varèse: An Interview," 455.

[50] Quoted in Mattis, "Varèse's Multimedia Conception of 'Déserts,'" 558.

[51] Quoted in Mattis, "Varèse's Multimedia Conception of 'Déserts,'" p. 561.

Magic Mountain in his descriptions of these magical, almost mythical, images of the landscape:

> Our almost daily meetings led to fascinating talks about the ecology of the region – how birds, animals, insects and plants had adapted to the heat and limited water supply, which consists of infrequent, spectacular but brief cloudbursts that for an hour seem about to wash everything away, and then very long droughts. There were trips to remote places such as Carr Canyon, the wild-bird paradise, but mainly it was right around the house that exotica (for an Easterner) could be seen – comic road runners [sic], giant [saguaros], flowering ocotillos, all sharing this special, dry world. It was indeed a kind of "magic mountain" and its specialness (for me) certainly encouraged the specialness (for me at that time) of the quartet as I worked on it during the fall and winter of '50 and the spring of '51.[52]

Carter's choice of words in this note is significant, as specific phrases he used in this program note to illustrate the ecology of the desert are the same ones he used to depict the musical events in his String Quartet No. 1, a work in which the process of interruption is one of the principal characteristics of the piece. For instance, Carter's account of the droughts that are interrupted by "spectacular but brief cloudbursts," manifest in his description of the second movement, Allegro scorrevole, which features a sound mosaic of "brief fragments, interrupted by a pause, again resumed, and finally interrupted by another outburst that forms the beginning of the Adagio."[53] Here, Carter refers to the form of the work, which comprises four movements (Fantasia, Allegro scorrevole, Adagio, and Variations) that flow into one another, yet the music flow is interrupted twice with dramatic pauses.[54]

While Carter does not use the actual sounds of nature in his piece, his representation of the desert in String Quartet No. 1 is metaphorical. Carter sought to abstractly portray the life of the desert in his piece, without explicit imitation, analogous to how Ezra Pound's notion of "absolute rhythm" offers a composer a way of communicating poetic meaning without resorting to excessive imitation.[55] Carter's approach also parallels William Carlos

---

[52] Carter, "String Quartets Nos. 1, 1951, and 2, 1959," in *Elliott Carter: Collected Essays and Lectures, 1937–1997*, 232. Carter likely makes a reference to Mann's novel, because its protagonist leaves his familiar life in Hamburg to visit his cousin in a sanatorium in the Swiss Alps. Throughout the novel, Mann evokes the magical and mythical atmosphere of the mountain.

[53] Carter, "String Quartets Nos. 1, 1951, and 2, 1959," 232; also see Emmery, *Compositional Process in Elliott Carter's String Quartets*, 25–26.

[54] See the formal diagram in Emmery, *Compositional Process in Elliott Carter's String Quartets*, 21–22.

[55] William Carlos Williams's poem, *The Desert Music*, inspired Steve Reich to compose a piece of the same title in 1983; for instance, see Coroniti, Jr., "Scoring the 'Absolute Rhythm' of Williams Carlos Williams: Steve Reich's 'The Desert Music.'" It is noteworthy that despite

Williams's observations during his own trip southwest to the desert of El Paso, Texas, and Juárez, Mexico in 1950, which resulted in his 1951 poem, *The Desert Music*, as he noted: "To copy nature is a spineless activity; it gives us a sense of our mere existence but hardly more than that. But to imitate nature involves the verb: we then ourselves become nature, and so invent an object which is an extension of the process."[56]

For Williams, a poet who had fascinated Carter since his college days,[57] imitating the desert and its music is also metaphorical. That is, as John Lowney observes, the music that Williams hears is an abstract "music of survival, subdued, distant, half/heard," the barely audible "desert music" that links his consciousness to the harsh desert landscape.[58] For Carter, too, the sounds of the desert are abstract in his Quartet: he sought to portray the experience of the passage of time and the life cycle in the desert, the drastic changes in the landscapes, and its diverse ecology: "Like the desert horizons I saw daily while it was being written, the First Quartet presents a continuous unfolding and changing of expressive characters – one woven into the other or emerging from it – on a large scale."[59]

Thus, String Quartet No. 1 features "many-layered contrasts of character,"[60] themes that emerge simultaneously with other themes, vanish at certain points, and reappear to start their cycles anew – constantly unfolding and changing. For Carter, applying the metaphor of desert ecology to his quartet was a way to engage with the meaning of events in their environment, which he had experienced after spending a year in the desert, trying to understand them, adapt to them, and replicate them musically.[61]

While "ecology" has become a crucial word today, as Jasper observes – "as the post-industrial parody of the wilderness, its wasteland" – it threatens, "in all its destructiveness, the fragile emptiness of deserted places."[62] This "frontier," Jasper continues, "is the line that is always being pushed back, across the desert, beyond which is the fabled country – the new promised land – of California and the West Coast with its City of Angels. [. . .] Yet, for others, the paradise lies not beyond the desert, but within."[63] Although the desert came to be associated with the "wasteland" in the verses of T. S. Eliot and was a metaphor for a personal

---

both Carter and Reich finding inspiration in Williams, the musical expression of the two composers is vastly different.

[56] Quoted in Myers, "Williams' Imitation of Nature in 'The Desert Music,'" 39.

[57] In 2022, Carter chose three poems by Williams for his song cycle for mezzo-soprano and orchestra, *Of Rewaking*.

[58] Quoted in Lowney, "Reading the Borders of 'The Desert Music,'" 69.

[59] Carter, "String Quartets Nos. 1, 1951, and 2, 1959," 231.

[60] Carter, "String Quartets Nos. 1, 1951, and 2, 1959," 234.

[61] Emmery, *Compositional Process in Elliott Carter's String Quartets*, 26.

[62] Jasper, *The Sacred Desert*, 74.

[63] Jasper, *The Sacred Desert*, 74.

struggle after overcoming an illness for William Carlos William, rather than associating it with death, dryness, and decay, Elliott Carter likened the Sonoran Desert to the "magical kingdom," a place that had remained protected from and immune to the noise and land pollution of the cities, a utopia.

The desert's landscape and ecology undoubtedly inspired Carter's ideas while working on his String Quartet No. 1. But perhaps even more importantly, the experience of "secluding" himself in the desert (even if not in a "monastic" way as described by Carter himself, his friends, and scholars) and being one with nature, put him in the company of those he greatly admired, explicitly Eliot, Williams, and Varèse, but also Henry David Thoreau, who spoke of the "absolute freedom" of Nature when he said, "Let me live where I will . . . on this side is the city, on that the wilderness, and ever I am leaving the city more and more, and withdrawing into the wilderness [. . .] in Wilderness is the preservation of the World."[64] Perhaps, like the dense monochrome paintings of Mark Rothko, an internal desert of extraordinary experience, where one finds oneself "neither inside nor outside, but both at once,"[65] Carter's String Quartet No. 1 came to represent such a depiction of the desert: a place where both internal and external times emerge, develop, and progress simultaneously.

Whether inspired by the mythological "magical kingdom" or the religious sacred desert, or perhaps the need to follow the footsteps of other modernists he greatly admired, or to truly seclude himself from the daily disturbances of the city to focus on developing his new musical language and expression, Carter's experience in the Sonoran Desert created one powerful narrative. It established Carter as a serious composer who exemplified an admirable dedication to the craft in the most arduous conditions. The narrative added another layer of depth to Carter's new ideas and the piece that resulted from this experience. It also created the myth surrounding Carter – about his "monastic seclusion" and consequent "conversion" from which a new composer emerged.

This compelling desert narrative thrust both Carter and his quartet to reach a special status – String Quartet No. 1 became the piece that separates Carter's compositional life into the "before" and "after." That is, only a couple of years earlier, Carter was writing pieces like his ballet *The Minotaur* (1947), a work that some critics even cautioned their readers against listening to because it disrupts the mythical narrative of the First Quartet. Schiff, for instance, writes of the ballet, "Perhaps, more than any other work, *The Minotaur* presents problems for anyone attempting to trace Carter's development."[66] Richard Franko Goldman's "pioneering" article on Carter's String Quartet No. 1 went even

---

[64] Thoreau, "Walking," in *Excursions: The Writings of Henry David Thoreau*, 267, 275. Also quoted in Jasper, *The Sacred Desert*, 6.

[65] Jasper, *The Sacred Desert*, 7.   [66] Schiff, *The Music of Elliott Carter*, 229.

further by stating: "*The Minotaur* is a good score, of which almost any American composer might be proud, but it is not altogether representative of the essential Carter style."[67] Thus the myth was solidified: Carter was no ordinary American composer, certainly not after the rebirth in the desert, and String Quartet No. 1 was the piece that exemplified Carter's essential style.

2 Intertextuality and Extramusical Associations

New York was a special place in the 1920s. Vividly described by Carol Oja, it "stood at a hub of action,"[68] becoming "the capital of the musical world."[69] In *Making Music Modern*, Oja captures what it meant to be in New York during this decade:

> To young creative artists of the 1920s, [New York] seemed to hold unprecedented charm and unlimited potential. As a talented new generation of American writers, musicians, and painters reached their maturity – ranging from Langston Hughes and Ernest Hemingway to Josephine Baker, Duke Ellington, Arthur Dove, and Georgia O'Keefe – it included composers who wrote music for the concert hall, most notably George Antheil, Aaron Copland, Henry Cowell, Ruth Crawford, George Gershwin, Roy Harris, Roger Sessions, William Grant Still, and Virgil Thomson. Riding a wave of postwar confidence, these young Americans staged a rebellion, challenging just everything around them. Women gained the vote, African Americans asserted creative leadership, and Americans suddenly realized that the world was paying serious attention to what they did. It was a time when any idea seemed realizable, when taking risks was the order of the day.[70]

David Schiff gives a similar account:

> In the first weeks of 1924, just after Carter turned fifteen, New York seemed to erupt with new music. On January 13, the International Composer's Guild Presented Varèse's *Octandre*. *Le sacre du printemps* had its Carnegie Hall premiere, with the Boston Symphony conducted by Pierre Monteux, on January 31. Paul Whiteman's "Experiment in Modern Music" at Aeolian Hall on February 11 launched Gershwin's *Rhapsody in Blue*. And that was just the beginning of the year.[71]

This is the New York in which Elliott Carter grew up. He recalls in one of his last interviews:

> When I was in high school, it was during the early period of the Soviet Union. As a result a lot of the children of the Soviet council, the people who worked

---

67 Richard Franko Goldman (1957), "The Music of Elliott Carter," *The Musical Quarterly* 43 (2): 159; quoted in Schiff (1998, 229).

68 Oja, *Making Music Modern*, 3.

69 Oja, *Making Music Modern*, 3. Oja cites Salzedo, "Outward Shows," 4.

70 Oja, *Making Music Modern*, 3.   71 Schiff, *Carter*, 43.

> in New York City, were at my school. I knew a whole world of this kind. I knew
> Eugene O'Neill's son, for instance, who was my best friend. So I was involved in
> this world of modernism very early on in my life. I got to know Varèse, who
> lived down the street here, when I was in high school. I knew him all his life from
> that time on. During this time of modernism, I didn't like Beethoven and all that
> stuff until much later. I thought all that was so old fashioned and so terrible.
> I would only go to concerts to stay for the modern music and leave.[72]

As a teenager, Carter attended the performances of new music in New York and
Boston, recalling that he was "old enough to have known a period when *The Rite
of Spring*, when played, chased everybody out of the hall," further explaining,
"You see, in those years, when I was in high school, and even in college,
Stokowski used to play Varèse around and occasionally in concerts, so I knew
all that stuff. That was all very exciting to me."[73]

In 1924, Carter met Charles Ives, who, recognizing his talents, took a liking
to young Carter and introduced him to notable figures in his circle, brought him
to concerts, and even wrote a recommendation for his studies at Harvard. In
1926, Carter began his undergraduate education in English, with secondary
concentrations in philosophy and classics.[74] Carter was rather disappointed
with his music education at Harvard, where his teachers included Walter
Piston and Gustav Holst, noting that no one there took an interest in new music:

> When I was in high school, I became interested in music by hearing pieces like
> *The Rite of Spring* and the music of Edgard Varèse. It was what got me interested
> in music. On the other hand, when I became a student, I found that all my teachers
> were so against the music that I'd been really interested in, so that if I wanted to
> learn anything about music, I had to learn what they wanted to teach.[75]

Further, he points directly to his Harvard education as a cause for composing in
the "Stravinsky-Hindemith" neoclassical style during the 1930s and 1940s,[76]
namely before the String Quartet No. 1, noting that the conservative environment
at Harvard also affected his tastes in music, but that luckily, he never lost his
desire or drive to write the music that he always liked: "As a result [of education at
Harvard], my tastes also changed, although I never gave up the idea that I would
eventually learn how to write the kind of advanced music that I do write now."[77]

---

⁷² Emmery, "An American Modernist: Teatime with Elliott Carter," 23–24.

⁷³ Emmery, "An American Modernist," 29, 28.

⁷⁴ Bernard, "Elliott Carter and the Modern Meaning of Time," 649.

⁷⁵ Emmery, *Elliott Carter Speaks*, 64.

⁷⁶ Maureen Carr argues that Stravinsky already started exhibiting traces of neoclassicism in 1914, the year after completing *The Rite of Spring* (see *After the Rite: Stravinsky's Path to Neoclassicism [1914–1925]*). Stravinsky continued writing in this style until 1951, when he turned to serialism.

⁷⁷ Emmery, *Elliott Carter Speaks*, 64.

Despite his dissatisfaction with music at Harvard, Carter was thrilled to live in Boston, where he would enjoy new music concerts at the Boston Symphony Orchestra, under the baton of Sergei Koussevitzky. As Carter remarks on his Boston experience, "I went to Harvard, for instance, not because of Harvard, but because the Boston Symphony was playing contemporary music under Koussevitzky. I heard a lot of concerts."[78]

Carter was introduced to the world of modernism through both music and literature. His earliest compositions, during the decades of the 1930s and 40s, are vocal works, which allowed him to combine his two passions – poetry and music.[79] Following a long pause, Carter returned to the genre of vocal music in 1975 with *A Mirror on Which to Dwell*, setting to music the works of his favorite modernist poets, such as Ezra Pound, William Carlos Williams, and T. S. Eliot.[80]

Growing up in New York in the age of modernism allowed Carter to see the many innovative ways artists found to appropriate ideas from other arts; as Jonathan Bernard notes, this was the time when "poetry borrowed from painting, painting from music, film from literature, and vice versa, and so on."[81] Carter not only set the lines of poetry to music but also seized the opportunity to incorporate extramusical ideas and use metaphors derived from other arts to describe the experience of time in his music, stating, "Time is the canvas on which you consider music to be presented, just as the spatial canvas of a painting furnishes the surface on which a painting is presented."[82] Such a visual metaphor of time is perpetuated in Schiff's discussion of the "cinematic continuity"[83] in String

---

[78] Emmery, "An American Modernist," 23.

[79] Carter's early songs and choral works, composed from 1936 through 1947, are set to texts by Ovid (*Tarantella*, 1937, rev. 1971), Robert Herrick (*Harvest Home*, 1937, rev. 1997; and *To Music*, 1937, rev. 1954), John Gay (*Let's Be Gay*, 1937), Emily Dickinson (*Heart Not So Heavy As Mine*, 1938; and *Musicians Wrestle Everywhere*, 1945), William Shakespeare (*Tell Me Where is Fancy Brad*, 1938), François Rabelais (*The Defense of Corinth*, 1941), Robert Frost (*Three Poems of Robert Frost*, 1942), Hart Crane (*Voyage*, 1942–43, rev. 1979), Walt Whitman (*Warble for Lilac Time*, 1943, rev. 1954), Mark Van Doren (*The Harmony of Morning*, 1944), and Allen Tate (*Emblems*, 1947). See www.elliottcarter.com/compositions/ for a complete list of Carter's compositions.

[80] See Emmery, "An American Modernist," 23. Carter used the texts by Elizabeth Bishop (*A Mirror on Which to Dwell*, 1975), John Ashbery (*Syringa*, 1978; and *Mad Regales*, 2007), Robert Lowell (*In Sleep, In Thunder*, 1981), John Hollander (*Of Challenge and of Love*, 1994), Eugenio Montale (*Tempo e Tempi*, 1998–99), William Carlos Williams (*Of Rewaking*, 2002), Wallace Stevens (*In the Distances of Sleep*, 2006; and *The American Sublime*, 2011), Charles Baudelaire (*La Musique*, 2007), Ezra Pound (*On Conversing with Paradise*, 2008), Louis Zukofsky (*Poems of Louis Zukofsky*, 2008), Marianne Moore (*What Are Years*, 2009), e.e.cummings (*A Sunbeam's Architecture*, 2010), and T. S. Eliot (*Three Explorations*, 2010–11). See www.elliottcarter.com/compositions for a complete list of Carter's compositions.

[81] Bernard, "Elliott Carter and the Modern Meaning of Time," 646.

[82] Carter, "Music and the Time Screen," 262.

[83] Schiff, *The Music of Elliott Carter*, 7.

Quartet No. 1: "Where the other quartets demand concentrated listening, the first calls for an expansive, imaginative response; the listener has to create a mental movie for which the quartet, so rich in its evocative powers and broad in its vision, is the soundtrack."[84]

While Carter had already introduced the metaphor of the desert and its ecology into String Quartet No. 1, he also started describing this work as having evolved from the many readings and his thinking on the topic of the human experience of time. Most notably, his influences were novelists, film-makers, and playwrights, such as Samuel Beckett, William S. Burroughs, Anton Chekhov, Jean Cocteau, Sergei Eisenstein, James Joyce, Marcel Proust, Rainer Maria Rilke, and Alain Robbe-Grillet, whose works, in his view, have encouraged musicians "to find new ways of dealing with perception, recognition, understanding, experience, and memory."[85] Further, at the time Carter was developing his new ideas in String Quartet No. 1, he was also avidly reading philosophical essays about the different ways of the experience of time, most notably the writings of Henri Bergson, Gisèle Brelet, Michel Butor, Charles Koechlin, and Pierre Suvchinsky. While the desert narrative already ushered in the extramusical meaning into Carter's String Quartet No. 1, incorporating modernist literature, film, and philosophy on time theories into the origin of the piece intensified the enigma and intrigue surrounding this work, and for Carter, enhanced his music with an added layer of prestige, positioning him as an especially intellectual and literary composer.

In addition to setting the verses of poetry to vocal music, Carter introduced literary sources to his instrumental music even before his String Quartet No. 1 – not only that his ballet, *Pocahontas* (1939), is based on the Native American saga of the Earth Mother, but the scenario by Lincoln Kirstein, who was the founder of Ballet Caravan, who had commissioned the ballet, included a verse from Hart Crane's poem, *The Bridge*:

> There was a bed of leaves and broken play;
> There was a veil upon you, Pocahontas, bride, –
> O Princess whose brown lap was virgin May;
> And bridal flanks and eyes hid tawny pride.[86]

---

[84] Schiff, *The Music of Elliott Carter*, 54.

[85] Carter, "La Musique sérielle aujourd'hui" (1965/94), 18. For a detailed analysis of how Carter applied the ideas from literature, film, and philosophical writings on time into his String Quartet No. 1, see Emmery, "Elliott Carter's First String Quartet: In Search of Proustian Time"; *Compositional Process in Elliott Carter's String Quartets*; Bernard, "Elliott Carter and the Modern Meaning of Time."

[86] Crane's long poem, *The Bridge*, was first published in 1930 by the Black Sun Press (Paris); this verse is quoted in Schiff, *The Music of Elliott Carter*, 15.

Although Carter did not inscribe this verse into the scenario himself – rather, as Schiff notes, he thought that Kirstein's citation was "merely an attempt to give the ballet some literary prestige"[87] – he did base his 1976 work, *A Symphony of Three Orchestras*, on the same poem. In addition to Crane, Carter also based his *Concerto for Orchestra* (1969), on *Vents* [Winds], a poem by Saint-John Perse.

Around the same time Carter was developing his ideas and introducing the extramusical into his instrumental works, a French philosopher, Étienne Souriau, was writing about the ways arts relate to one another. He specifically examined the question about "inspirations" and "transformations" from one art form into another and pondered if there is a risk that such "representation of a representation"[88] would appear as a merely derivative response. "There is something odd, and even disturbing, in second-hand inspiration, sought in the works of someone else, and sought in an art form of which the aims and the means are very different from those which characterize poetry. Is this really legitimate? Is this truly useful and fruitful?"[89]

In her work on musical ekphrasis, Siglind Bruhn offers insight into the notion of such "transformations" or new representations in another sign system. While the concept of ekphrasis first appears in the Roman Greek period to refer primarily to a literary work that derives from a visual work of art,[90] Bruhn has expanded and adapted the term "musical ekphrasis" to signify a relation between music and other adjoining artistic fields.[91] For Bruhn, thus, Carter's use of verses by Crane and Perse, just like Ravel's reference to the three poems of Aloysius Bertrand in *Gaspard de la nuit* (1908), is not just a matter of applying a vague or impressionistic "program." Rather, in these musical compositions, a transformation of a message from one medium into another takes place.[92] Such transformations occur when composers capture the content, form, imagery, and suggested symbolic signification from a poem (or another art) into their compositions. In these compositions, such connections

---

87 Schiff, *The Music of Elliott Carter*, 15.

88 Bruhn, *Musical Ekphrasis: Composers Responding to Poetry and Painting*, xv.

89 In French: "il y a de bizarre, et même d'inquiétant, dans le fait d'une inspiration de seconde main, cherchée dans les œuvres d'autrui, et cherchée dans un art dont les buts et les moyens sont très différents de ceux qui caractérisent l'art poétique. Est-ce vraiment légitime? Est-ce vraiment utile et fécond?" (Souriau, *La poésie française et la peinture*, 6).

90 See Hilewicz, "Reciprocal Interpretations of Music and Painting: Representation Types in Schuller, Tan, and Davies after Paul Klee," for the history of the term and its applications to music.

91 Also see Goehr, "How to Do More with Words: Two Views of (Musical) Ekphrasis" for the application of ekphrasis within the discussion of music.

92 Bruhn, *Musical Ekphrasis*, xvi.

to an extramusical stimulus allow listeners to fully understand a piece only when appreciating it as a transmedialization of a corresponding poem (or another work of art).[93]

Musical ekphrasis in Carter's String Quartet No. 1 is more nuanced and complex. Unlike *A Symphony of Three Orchestras* or *Concerto for Orchestra*, which were directly inspired by poetry verses, the influence for the Quartet was drawn from intangible ideas in modernist literature and film to portray musically the nonlinear experience of time. Although, as discussed previously, Carter was stirred by the desert landscape and listened to its ecology, it was not just the visual aspect of the desert that appealed to Carter. Rather, he was also intrigued by the cycle of events unfolding in this ecology, for he writes, "Like the desert horizons I saw daily [...] the First Quartet presents a continuous unfolding and changing of expressive characters – one woven into the other or emerging from it."[94] Thus, for Carter, the concept of cycles (and circularity) and the psychology of the passage of time, that is, the temporal aspect of music, were most essential while developing his new ideas in the Quartet.

The temporal aspect of music continued to intensify for Carter after the Quartet – from the 1980s onward, Carter structured virtually all of his music according to the principle of long-range polyrhythms – rhythmic relationships that guide the structure of an entire composition.[95] The depth of his thinking on this topic is also revealed in the essays and lectures he had written over several decades, including "The Rhythmic Basis of American Music" (1955),[96] "The Time Dimension in Music" (1965),[97] "Music and the Time Screen" (1976),[98] and "Time Lecture" (1965/94),[99] as well as his unpublished notes (housed at the Paul Sacher Stiftung) about his thoughts on the topic of time and music.

---

[93] Bruhn, *Musical Ekphrasis*, xvi–xvii. For more on this topic, also see *Images and Ideas in Modern French Piano Music: The Extra-Musical Subtext in Piano Works by Ravel, Debussy, and Messiaen.*

[94] Carter, "String Quartets Nos. 1, 1951, and 2, 1959," 231.

[95] For more on Carter's long-range polyrhythms, see Bernard, "The Evolution of Elliott Carter's Rhythmic Practice"; Coulembier, "Elliott Carter's Structural Polyrhythms in the 1970s: 'A Mirror on Which to Dwell'"; Emmery, "Rhythmic Process in Elliott Carter's Fourth String Quartet"; Emmery, *Compositional Process in Elliott Carter's String Quartets*; Jenkins, "After the Harvest: Carter's Fifth String Quartet and the Late Late Style"; Link, "Long-Range Polyrhythms in Elliott Carter's Recent Music"; A. Mead, "Time Management"; Poudrier, "Toward a General Theory of Polymeter: Polymetric Potential and Realization in Elliott Carter's Solo and Chamber Instrumental Works after 1980."

[96] See Carter, "The Rhythmic Basis of American Music" (1955).

[97] See Carter, "La Musique sérielle aujourd'hui."

[98] See Carter, "Music and the Time Screen."

[99] See Carter, "La Musique sérielle aujourd'hui."

These essays and especially the notes tell us not only that the concept of time permeated Carter's thoughts, but how they concretely influenced his ideas in String Quartet No. 1. In 1970, two decades after he had written the First Quartet, Carter offered a detailed explanation about how Jean Cocteau's 1930 avant-garde film, *Le Sang d'un poète* [The Blood of a Poet], gave him the idea for the structure of his Quartet. That is, Cocteau frames the entire movie with a shot of a collapsing chimney – we see the beginning of the collapse in the opening scene of the film and then its disintegration at the end (Figure 2). Carter applies this technique to the form of his quartet by framing the work with two solo cadenzas – the first one by the cello at the beginning of the quartet that is continued by the first violin at the very end of the piece (Figure 3), between which the music unfolds in the work's "internal time" as he explains:

> The general plan was suggested by Jean Cocteau's film *Le Sang d'un poète*, in which the entire dream-like action is framed by an interrupted slow-motion shot of a tall brick chimney in an empty lot being dynamited. Just as the chimney begins to fall apart, the shot is broken off and the entire movie follows, after which the shot of the chimney is resumed at the point it left off, showing its disintegration in mid-air, and closing the film with its collapse on the ground. A similar interrupted continuity is employed in this quartet's starting with a cadenza for cello alone that is continued by the first violin alone at the very end. On one level, I interpret Cocteau's idea (and my own) as establishing the difference between external time (measured by the falling chimney, or the cadenza) and internal dream time (the main body of the work) – the dream time lasting but a moment of external time but from the dreamer's point of view, a long stretch.[100]

Figure 2 Jean Cocteau, *Le Sang d'un poète* (1930); **(a)** the opening frame of the collapsing chimney, 02:02; **(b)** the closing frame of the collapsing chimney, 50:07.

---

[100] Carter, "String Quartets Nos. 1, 1951, and 2, 1959," 233.

Figure 3 Elliott Carter, String Quartet No. 1 (1950–51) Copyright © 1956 (Renewed) by Associated Music Publishers, Inc. International copyright secured. All rights reserved. Used by permission; **(a)** the opening cadenza, cello solo, *Fantasia*, mm. 1–12; **(b)** the closing cadenza, violin solo, *Variations*, mm. 490–504.

However, other than mentioning literary authors in his lectures and essays, Carter was less clear about how the various literary sources actually helped him derive and transform the ideas in his Quartet.[101] Fortunately, his unpublished notes shed more light on this topic. Most notably, Carter was influenced by Marcel Proust's *À la recherche du temps perdu*,[102] which was (posthumously)

---

[101] In my previous studies on Carter's String Quartet No. 1, I discuss in detail some of the Proustian techniques Carter used in his First Quartet (see "Elliott Carter's First String Quartet: In Search of Proustian Time" and *Compositional Process in Elliott Carter's String Quartets*). Also see Bernard, "Elliott Carter and the Modern Meaning of Time," for a brief discussion of Proustian memory and its impact on Carter, as well as the analogies of Carter's compositional techniques to James Joyce's *Ulysses* and Sergei Eisenstein's cinematographic and montage techniques in *Battleship Potemkin* and *Ten Days that Shook the World*.

[102] Marcel Proust (1871–1922) began working on his novel in 1909 and it would take him the rest of his life to complete all seven volumes: Vol. 1 (1913): *Du côté de chez Swann* (Swann's Way); Vol. 2 (1919): *À l'ombre des jeunes filles en fleurs* (Within a Budding Grove); Vol. 3 (1920–21): *Le Côté de*

being released in Paris at the time when Carter was living in Paris, allowing him to read the first edition of the novel in French, and then several more times throughout his life.[103] Many of his notes reference Proust as a direct influence on his music. As I have shown in my earlier work on Carter, even though the discussion of Proust does not appear in the published versions of the essays, Carter initially planned to start his "The Time Dimension in Music" lecture with a discussion of "Proustian Time."[104] Further, his other unpublished notes spell out Proustian techniques and how he transformed those into his First Quartet, and also how they, generally, changed his thinking about music. In one note, Carter writes,

> Our conception of, so to speak, linear progress of time, of the importance of time has undergone a very profound change in the course of the past 50 years, due partly to the writings of various novelists, dramatists and psychologists, also to the movies, to the notion of "time-saving" methods, and to changes in speed of travel of communication.
>
> Marcel Proust presented the most striking statement of this in the last volume of A la Recherche.[105]

As Carter jots down several passages from Proust's novel in French, he also offers his own assessment on the topic of "Proustian time" (while also referencing Edgar Allan Poe, Rilke, and Chekhov) and how these literary techniques are reflected in his String Quartet No. 1. He writes:

1. The meaning of the time-dimension as seen in our time: Proust

    (a) a large stored composite of many impressions, feelings, thoughts, skills which our memory has knitted together in many different. [sic] Sometimes according to what may seem like inconsequential or irrelevant tags which may plumb the very depths of our thoughts as the famous madeleine or the doorbell heard in his childhood, that were the touchstones for Proust of his entire vision of life.

    (b) This collection of memory impressions is in one sense the source of our identity as Proust said: [...] and the passing of time as it partially obliterates our memory robs us of our own identity – Rilke.

Guermantes (The Guermantes Way); Vol. 4 (1921–22): *Sodome et Gomorrhe* (Cities of the Plain); Vol. 5 (1923): *La Prisonnière* (The Captive); Vol. 6 (1925): *La Fugitive/Albertine disparue* (The Fugitive); Vol. 7 (1927): *Le Temps retrouvé* (Time Regained). Republished in 1981, *Remembrance of Things Past*, 3 vols., trans. C. K. Scott Moncrieff and T. Kilmartin (New York: Random House).

[103] Even shortly before he died in 2012, Carter revealed that he had started reading the novel once again. See Emmery, "An American Modernist," 23.

[104] See Emmery, *Compositional Process in Elliott Carter's String Quartets*, ch. 1, especially pp. 10–18.

[105] Elliott Carter Collection, Text manuscripts, "The Time Dimension in Music" (Paul Sacher Stiftung, Basel).

Similarly the passing of time can also modify and change our memory store and revise its meaning and emphasis.

(c) this is very obvious, and in the present century many writers besides Rilke and Proust have considered the question of time from special points of view. For instance, the influence of Chekov's plays with its new concept of continuity was crucial. For him, linear plot following in a casual order was discarded as it was in Proust for contextual or concentric actions. Characters are shown each in their special way, revealed one after the other reactiong [sic] to special situations – each of which could have given rise to the plot of a play but which as Chekov presents them are passed by, for another revelation. There is a similar method in the "epiphanies" in Joyce's work. In fact, Ulysses and Finnegan's [sic] Wake the complex layers of consciousness bring different ideas and experiences into focus one after the other relating them somehow to the total background of the character's situation or as, in the case of Finnegan, the entire range of human experience. So that experience, the storage of events in time is constantly referred to and illumines in various ways, comically, or tragically the events of the present.

Now without this background of experience, of memories, both as human being and as listeners to music it is obvious that a work of music can have very little meaning to its listener.[106]

Following these thoughts on the treatment of time in modernist literary works, Carter proceeds to explain more concretely how he adapted these ideas while writing his String Quartet No. 1 (and in his works since 1950, generally).

My works therefore have been primarily concerned with their extensibility in time and in each work a new a different approach was used.

[…] In 1949, I became very interested in developing mosaic texture, made up of small neutral bits of musical material like tessera in a mosaic that because of their ways of being assembled gave varying characters and impressions. …

[…]

The mosaic idea was one way of uniting together elements from different parts and characters of the work [into] new frames – Another as seen in my first [quartet] where a four part texture brings together four of the important speeds, themes and characters of the work simultaneously.

[…]

On a larger scale, I have found large patterns of time opportunities that extend through an entire work.

---

[106] Elliott Carter Collection, Text manuscripts, "The Time Dimension in Music" (Paul Sacher Stiftung, Basel).

> The opening of and close of the 3rd movement of my 1st qt. states a slow theme in
> the 'cello which is heard repeatedly throughout the work each time faster until it
> reaches the point heard on the second excerpt. Meanwhile, many other themes
> have been introduced which also become faster at different rates of speed.[107]

While Carter does not directly translate any lines from literature into music in the String Quartet No. 1, intertextuality and extramusical associations in this work are quite evident. Specifically, Carter transforms Cocteau's formal scheme into the structure of the quartet and translates literary techniques into his compositional techniques. This is reflected in Carter's development of musical characters – perhaps akin to Proust's development of "the little phrase" in his novel, which undergoes transformations as do places, objects, and ideas associated with each character[108] – but also the simultaneity of themes, multiple speeds of different musical layers, and the circularity of themes that start, spiral, and vanish, just to start anew. Thus, Carter found in these artists a method to focus on the time dimension in music, or to reflect on new ways of structuring and thinking about time in the twentieth century, leading him to conclude that the most compelling aspect of music is time – more specifically, recognizing that within each present point, there are infinite points in the past, and memory plays a key role in relating all events in time and space.

Situating himself among the notable modernists of his time was essential to Carter and the early reception of his Quartet. As he noted previously in reference to the appearance of Crane's poem in the scenario for *Pocahontas*, likening his music to literature added some "literary prestige." By referencing Proust, Joyce, and Cocteau, among others, as his direct influences for his String Quartet No. 1, Carter effectively elevated the reputation of the work, as the quartet is seldom discussed without placing it in the company of notable twentieth-century modernist writers and artists. Hence, Carter placed his String Quartet No. 1 at the center of most notable modern artistic achievements, during a turning point in the American (musical) postwar period.

3 Musical Borrowings and Homages

In his 1957 review of the Walden Quartet's recording of Carter's String Quartet No. 1, George Rochberg wrote:

> If one compares this quartet to other contemporary quartets – Bartók's,
> Schoenberg's, Berg's – one immediately recognizes it as a marker,
> a milestone towards which the contemporary quartet has been moving; this

---

[107] Elliott Carter Collection, Text manuscripts, "The Time Dimension in Music" (Paul Sacher Stiftung, Basel).

[108] For more on the transformations of "the little phrase" in Proust's novel, see Emmery, "Elliott Carter's First String Quartet: In Search of Proustian Time," 24–27.

> despite the debt it owes to all the others and in spite of its own limitations. . . .
> It would not be difficult to show how much the *Allegro scorrevole* (the second
> movement) and its prior preparation at the end of the first movement marked
> *Fantasia*, owes to the *Allegro misterioso* of Berg's *Lyric Suite* (or those
> movements in the Bartók quartets whose texture is similar in design, whose
> musical content is equally whimsical or fantastic). Or how this passage here,
> that one there evokes the quality of similar passages by Bartók; or how certain
> sonorities and attitudes of the Schoenberg Trio seem to cast their shadow.[109]

Rochberg's review, which precedes Goldman's analysis of the quartet, set
a precedent for all subsequent reviews and scholarship on this work, effectively
creating a narrative that puts the discussion of Carter's quartet in direct dialogue
with those of Bartók, Berg, and Schoenberg, and later of Ruth Crawford. While
the earliest reviews of the first performances of the quartet merely mention
Bartók and Schoenberg – such as Steinberg's observation that not since Bartók's
Fourth Quartet has there been a significant addition to the quartet literature or
Frankenstein's statement that by hearing Carter's quartet it was evident that
"Carter has lived in the age of Bartók and Schönberg"[110] – Rochberg directly
compared Carter's quartet to the notable works of the leading composers of
contemporary music at that time. Thus, by situating Carter's quartet along
Bartók's quartets, Schoenberg's Trio, and Berg's *Lyric Suite*, Rochberg created
a narrative that placed Carter deservingly in the company of the most notable
and respected composers at the time, concluding that such assimilation, while
creating one's own musical expression, is only logical:

> Such associations tell us only something of what Carter is drawn to, what he
> believes in and whom he follows chronologically; to take them as an indica-
> tion of the worth of the work would be to deny him his marked powers of
> assimilation and capacity to re-shape the content of his personal musical
> world.[111]

Soon after Rochberg's review, Goldman's essay on Carter's music solidified the
idea that, unlike other young composers who were running out of original ideas
and unsuccessfully imitating others, Carter stood out among all of them as an
example of the most original, exciting, and "first-class" American composer,
who managed to both assimilate the best these "masters" had to offer, while also
distancing himself from his predecessors to give us something quite new:

> The 1950's have been uneventful. New works appear with regularity, but they
> say little new, and in some case give evidence that the original vein is worked

---

[109]   Rochberg, "Review, Elliott Carter: Quartet by Elliott Carter," 130–31.
[110]   Frankenstein, "California String Quartet Offers Concert Eloquence," 25.
[111]   Rochberg, "Review, Elliott Carter: Quartet by Elliott Carter," 131.

> out. The younger composers for the most part are imitating their elders
> without much luck; the young Sessionses, Coplands, and Schumans are
> writing neutrally and eclectically; the middle-aged Weberns, Stravinskys,
> Bartóks, and Hindemiths for the most part are doing as well as they always
> do, which is not quite well enough. It is hard to think of any American
> composer under the age of thirty-five who seems absolutely first-class. [...]
>
> The one composer of importance who has recently come to the fore is
> Elliott Carter, and his music represents what is perhaps the most significant
> American development of the last ten years.[112]

Goldman's overwhelming and hyperbolic support for Carter is apparent; his
statement that the 1950s have been "uneventful" until Carter's String Quartet
No. 1 took the stage is rather subjective and arguable. In Europe, Pierre Boulez's
Polyphonie X (1950–51) and *Structures* (1952) were premiered during this
period, followed by Karlheinz Stockhausen's *Punkte* and *Spiel* (1952). In the
United States, John Cage debuted his indeterminate music, first with *Imaginary
Landscape No. 4* (1951), and then with the application of *I Ching* to derive chance
operations in *Music of Changes* (1951), and the ground-breaking *4'33"* (1952),
while Conlon Nancarrow's *Rhythm Study No. 1* for Player Piano (1949–50) was
published in 1951, just to name a few notable musical achievements of the early
1950s. Morton Feldman, for instance, describes this decade as one of the most
productive and creative periods in the arts because of the "freedom of people to be
themselves," exemplified by Mark Rothko, in his view, an artist "who was free to
do only one thing – to make a Rothko – and did so over and over again."[113] As
Feldman distinctly describes the bustling artistic scene in New York City at this
time, surrounded by painters (such as Philip Guston, Willem de Kooning, Robert
Rauschenberg, and Sonja Sekula), sculptors (Max Ernst, David Hare, and
Richard Lippold), writers (Frank O'Hara), performers (David Tudor), and composers (Cage, Henry Cowell, and Pierre Boulez), among many others, the 1950s
could hardly be conceived as "uneventful." Nonetheless, Goldman proclaims
Carter's quartet as the most important American musical accomplishment of the
decade: "The 1951 String Quartet [...] is almost without doubt the most important and imposing accomplishment of American music in the last decade; it has
aroused the keenest interest and discussion in both Europe and the United
States."[114]

Joseph Kerman's 1957 review of Walden Quartet's Columbia recording
likened Carter's quartet to another of history's "greats": "When Carter makes
a solemn unaccompanied *da capo* of the opening of his first movement as a final

---

[112] Goldman, "The Music of Elliott Carter," 151–52.
[113] Feldman, "Give My Regards to Eighth Street," 99. I would like to thank the anonymous
reviewer for this insight.
[114] Goldman, "The Music of Elliott Carter," 162.

variation in his last movement, the result is no more than a paradox. One thinks idly of the finale in Brahms' Clarinet Quintet."[115]

This type of adulation for Carter's quartet, while assigning the work a certain prestige by comparing it to renowned figures continued even in more contemporary reviews. For instance, in 2018, David Schiff noted that by successfully distancing himself from Schoenberg, Carter was "the emancipator of musical discourse" and the "inheritor not only to the entire tradition that culminated in Schoenberg's music, but to other traditions as well."[116] For Schiff, Carter was ostensibly the greatest innovator of the century, who declared himself "not just the equal of the Einstein of twentieth-century music but his rightful successor."[117] It is virtually impossible to find a piece of scholarship on Carter's String Quartet No. 1 that does not mimic the same observations set forth by Rochberg and Goldman, as illustrated in Schiff's reiteration that Carter's quartets continued Bartók's great trajectory of the genre: "Carter's five quartets [. . .] take up the genre of the modernist string quartet where Bartók had left off. Like the Bartók quartets, Carter's are virtuosic and meditative, emotionally intense yet structurally rigorous. Like Beethoven's and Bartók's, they may be seen to form a spiritual autobiography."[118]

In his discussion of the String Quartet No. 1, specifically, Schiff continues with the comparison of this work to Schoenberg, Beethoven, Berg, and Bartók, and also Ruth Crawford, an American "ultramodernist":

> The First Quartet approaches the scale of Beethoven's op. 127 or Schoenberg's op. 7. It owes little to the classical tradition, though it is clearly indebted to the examples of Berg's *Lyric Suite*, Bartók's Fourth Quartet, and in particular, Ruth Crawford's String Quartet.[119] [. . .] The "scherzo" sections [in Allegro scorrevole] are reminiscent of the Allegro misterioso of Berg's *Lyric Suite* while the "trio" sections suggest, in passing, the "Tenebroso" passages of that work.[120]

Jonathan Bernard also compares the sheer size of the work to Beethoven and Schoenberg: "There is, first of all, the matter of sheer length: approximately thirty-five to forty minutes depending on the performance, thus demanding the unbroken attention of listeners on the scale comparable to that of Schoenberg's first quartet or one of the late Beethoven quartets."[121]

Similarly, Felix Meyer and Anne Shreffler note that "Carter's quartet shares with Schoenberg's *First String Quartet* its length, extensively contrapuntal

---

[115] Kerman, "American Music: The Columbia Series," 423.
[116] Schiff, *Carter*, 93.
[117] Schiff, *Carter*, 93.
[118] Schiff, *The Music of Elliott Carter*, 53.
[119] Schiff, *The Music of Elliott Carter*, 55.
[120] Schiff, *The Music of Elliott Carter*, 64.
[121] Bernard, "The String Quartets of Elliott Carter," 239.

texture, and wide expressive range," and that its formal design "recalls the continuous, interlocking four movements of Schoenberg's quartet."[122] Dörte Schmidt confirms the parallels, stating that "the references in the First Quartet reveal a particular interest in Bartók and the Viennese School, in keeping with Carter's reorientations in the late 1940s."[123]

Thus, it would appear that Carter evoked the sounds and grandiose scale of Beethoven, Schoenberg, Berg, Bartók, Crawford, and Debussy,[124] but had also successfully distanced himself from all of these composers to make a new statement. Shreffler, however, reveals that Carter derived many of the "distinctive features" that characterize his String Quartet No. 1 – namely, "the differentiation of voices, the exploration of clusters as timbre, and the generation of rhythmic processes" – directly from Crawford's 1931 String Quartet.[125] Nancy Yunhwa Rao substantiates this claim by tracing the evolution of Carter's dissonant writing to Crawford.[126]

The evocation of the "masters" of the earlier generations in less critical reviews may be understood as a tribute, a way for Carter to pay homage to the composers he greatly admired and whose music helped him shape his own musical expression. The comparison to Schoenberg is perhaps the most significant because it similarly justifies the complexity of Carter's new language in the quartet. As the work's early critics noted, the quartet is "extremely long" and features "rhythmic complexities" (Frankenstein), and its sheer difficulty makes Schoenberg seem not more difficult than Kuhlau or Clementi (Glock). However, these critics also recognized that such complexity emerged not for the sake of just being difficult, but from Carter's need to express his new ideas about rhythm, harmony, counterpoint, form, time, and characters he was developing at that time. Even though Carter famously exclaimed, "To hell

---

[122] Meyer and Shreffler, *Elliott Carter: A Centennial Portrait in Letters and Documents*, 101.

[123] Schmidt, "'I Try to Write Music That Will Appeal to an Intelligent Listener's Ear,'" 172.

[124] In his most recent work on Carter, Schiff notes the "echoes of Bartók's Fourth Quartet, Berg's Lyric Suite, and Debussy's Violin Sonata, and on a conceptual level at least two implied precursors: Schoenberg's String Quartet No. 1, op. 7, and Ruth Crawford's String Quartet [...] particularly its first movement" can be heard in Carter's First Quartet (see Schiff, *Carter*, 94). Sketches for Carter's Second String Quartet (1959) indicate that Carter was directly influenced by Bartók and Anton Webern. In one sketch for the fourth movement, Carter inscribes, "For Bartók," and also found among the folios of sketches for this work is Carter's own partial transcription of Webern's *Bagatelle for String Quartet*, no. 6, op. 9. See Emmery, *Compositional Process in Elliott Carter's String Quartets*, ch. 2. Carter spoke of Debussy's influence on his music, stating "I wrote a work myself that illustrated what I saw in Debussy—Sonata for Flute, Oboe, Cello, and Harpsichord. [...] The Sonata attempted to find a way of dealing with this special flow of thoughts that Debussy also had" (Emmery, *Elliott Carter Speaks*, 45).

[125] Shreffler, "Elliott Carter and His America," 49–50.

[126] Rao, "*Allegro scorrevole* in Carter's First String Quartet."

with the public and with the performers too,"[127] Glock concludes that Carter's quartet does more than subject the audience to "forty-five minutes of admirable hell." Thus, Carter sought to restructure the rhythmic expression in his music not only because he wanted to write a composition that would be compelling to him without compromising any of his new ideas for the sake of satisfying the audience or performers but, more importantly, because he saw it as a necessary step in the logical path of music discourse. Similarly, Schoenberg also described his method of composing with twelve tones as growing out of necessity.

Carter's path to new ideas was indeed an arduous one, taking seven years to formalize in String Quartet No. 1. On some level, it parallels Schoenberg's twelve-year process of developing his method of composing with twelve tones.[128] For both composers, the challenge was not only about developing new ways of expressing musical ideas but also about the acceptance of the method. Schoenberg decided to keep silent for two years, anticipating resistance and confusion,[129] while Carter, fully aware of the complexity of his new musical language, was concerned about whether the piece would ever be performed or understood by the audience.[130] To justify the difficulty of his new harmonic method, Schoenberg reminded us of Brahms and how his music was deemed too difficult and incomprehensible at the time: "Younger listeners will probably be unaware that at the time of Brahms's death this [Cello] sonata [in F major] was still very unpopular and was considered indigestible. Older listeners will no doubt remember that for twenty years the Violin Concerto was thought to be unplayable, unviolinistic, despite Joachim's advocacy."[131]

By bringing up the progressive music of Brahms, Schoenberg in effect established his own credibility and justified that he deservingly carried forward the lineage of history's most significant composers. Hence, Carter's comparison to Schoenberg is rather noteworthy as it now puts Carter directly as the carrier of this extraordinary lineage, establishing Carter's own authority and thus his well-deserved placement in the musical canon.

---

[127] Edwards, *Flawed Words and Stubborn Sounds*, 35.

[128] Schoenberg, "Composition with Twelve-Tones (1)": "After many unsuccessful attempts during a period of approximately twelve years, I laid the foundations for a new procedure in musical construction which seemed fitted to replace those structural differences provided formerly by tonal harmonies. I called this procedure Method of Composing with Twelve Tones Which are Related Only with One Another," 218.

[129] Schoenberg, "Schoenberg's Tone-Rows (1936)," 213.

[130] See Emmery, *Compositional Process in Elliott Carter's String Quartets*, 8–9.

[131] Schoenberg, "The Orchestral Variations, Op. 31: A Radio Talk," 29.

Carter himself directly contributed to the intrigue and reception of his String Quartet No. 1 by explaining that he used direct quotations in this work to pay homage to the composers whose rhythmic innovations inspired him to pursue his own ideas – Charles Ives and Conlon Nancarrow. Carter writes:

> This quartet, for instance, quotes the opening theme of Ives's First Violin Sonata, first played by the cello in its lowest register after each of the other instruments has come in near the beginning. A rhythmic idea from Conlon Nancarrow's First Rhythm Study is quoted at the beginning of the Variations. These two composers, both through their music and their conversation, had been a great help to me in imagining this work and were quoted in homage.[132]

Indeed, the opening theme of Ives's First Violin Sonata is quoted by the cello in Carter's Fantasia movement, starting in m. 27 (Figure 4). Carter's choice of this particular selection is peculiar – the theme opens with an F-minor triad, a type of harmonic sonority Carter sought to avoid in his String Quartet No. 1.[133] Further, the theme is not quite discernible as it is neither a prominent theme in Ives's oeuvre nor is it necessarily noticeable in Carter's quartet – the theme is buried within the busy texture of four simultaneous themes at different speeds, articulations, rhythms, and characters.[134] Perhaps, quoting Ives was not so much of a homage as it was Carter's public apology to his mentor, whom he openly humiliated in his brutal review of the *Concord Sonata* in *Modern Music,* following the piece's first performance in New York in 1939 by John Kirkpatrick. In his scathing review, Carter wrote:

Figure 4 (a) Charles Ives, Violin Sonata No. 1, m. 1.

---

[132] Carter, "String Quartets Nos. 1, 1951, and 2, 1959," 233.

[133] David Schiff has said that Carter initially avoided the all-interval tetrachord (0137) because, at that time, it appeared too tonally suggestive due to its subset of a minor triad (*The Music of Elliott Carter*, 64). However, it should be noted that Carter uses both (0137) and (0146) all-interval tetrachords in his String Quartet No. 1, although the latter sonority is more prevalent.

[134] Anne Shreffler posits that Carter's choice of Ives's First Violin Sonata is significant in that it is personal, as this was one of the first scores by Ives that Carter owned, which Ives gave to him when he was a student at Harvard; see Shreffler, "Elliott Carter and His America," 53.

Figure 4 (b) Elliott Carter, String Quartet No. 1, Fantasia, mm. 27–30: musical quotation of Ives's First Violin Sonata in the cello. Copyright © 1956 (Renewed) by Associated Music Publishers, Inc. International copyright secured. All rights reserved. Used with permission.

In form and aesthetic it is basically conventional, not unlike the Liszt Sonata, full of the paraphernalia of the overdressy sonata school, cyclical themes, contrapuntal development sections that lead nowhere, constant harmonic movement which does not clarify the form, and dramatic rather than rhythmical effects. Because of the impressionistic intent of most of the music, the conventional form seemed to hamper rather than aid, resulting in unnecessary, redundant repetitions of themes, mechanical transitions uncertain in their direction; unconvincing entrances of material; dynamics which have no relation to the progress of the piece. Behind all this confused texture there is a lack of logic which repeated hearing can never clarify, as they do for instance in the works of Bartók and Berg. The rhythms are vague and give no relief to the more expressive sections, and the much touted dissonant harmonies are helter-skelter, without great musical sense of definite progression. The aesthetic is naïve, often too naïve to express serious thoughts, frequently depending on quotation of well-known American tunes, with little comment, possibly charming, but certainly trivial. As a whole, the work cannot be said to fill out the broad, elevated design forecast in the composer's prefaces.[135]

This blistering review permanently strained Carter's relationship with Ives, who only a decade earlier had written a letter of recommendation for Carter to the Dean of Harvard University. In that letter, Ives described Carter as an "exceptional boy . . . of good character" and noted his "reliability, industry, and a sense of

---

[135] Carter, "The Case of Mr. Ives (1939)," 89; also quoted in Schiff, *The Music of Elliott Carter,* 16–17.

honor."[136] Yet, there was nothing honorable in Carter's public discredit of Ives. Perhaps, Carter resented that Lawrence Gilman, a critic for the *New York Herald Tribune*, had just proclaimed the *Concord Sonata* "the greatest music composed by an American, and the most deeply and essentially American in impulse and implication."[137] After all, this review was not written by the "reborn" Carter of the String Quartet No. 1 era, but the Carter who composed *Pocahontas*, a piece so ill-received that it prompted Copland to write a letter to Koussevitzky to say, "I need not tell you about the quality of the piece as you can see that for yourself."[138] Still elated from his recent studies with Nadia Boulanger in Paris, Carter was looking for ways to find his own voice and place in America upon his return from Paris and to make a mark in the trajectory of American modernism. Before he would compose his landmark String Quartet No. 1, which would just achieve this goal, Carter asserted his dominance through this cruel review of Ives's Sonata, a deed he would come to regret his entire life.

Even though Carter tried to redeem himself by writing two other essays about Ives in the short period after – "Ives Today: His Vision and Challenge" (1944) and "An American Destiny" (1946),[139] he certainly drew much attention to his admiration for and friendship with Ives by quoting Ives in his String Quartet No. 1. Thus, the use of the musical quotation of an Ives theme is just as much a humble apology as it is an homage to a great friend. Both of these interpretations created an astonishing narrative for Carter's Quartet, as an homage to Ives became inextricable from the discussion of the quartet itself. The impact of the Ives quotation on the reception and our understanding of Carter's quartet is quite powerful, more so than any other comparison of this work, as vividly illustrated by Meyer's and Shreffler's statement that "if Schoenberg, Berg ... and Bartók were the quartet's European ancestors, its American grandfather was Ives, whose influence Carter explicitly acknowledged by using the head motive from Ives's *First Violin Sonata* as one of the main themes of the first movement."[140]

The circumstances surrounding the Nancarrow musical quotation are even more intriguing. In his notes for the String Quartet No. 1, Carter wrote that the beginning of the Variations movement quotes a theme from Nancarrow's *Rhythm Study No. 1*, a statement that has been taken *de facto* by Carter scholars.

---

[136] Felix Meyer and Anne C. Shreffler, *Elliott Carter: A Centennial Portrait in Letters and Documents*, 25.

[137] Quoted in Schiff, *The Music of Elliott Carter*, 16.

[138] Copland and Perlis, *Copland: 1900 through 1942*, 283; quoted in Schiff, *The Music of Elliott Carter*, 18.

[139] Carter also wrote "Charles Ives Remembered" in 1974 and "Documents of a Friendship with Ives" in 1975, and throughout his life continued to speak of both his admiration for and issues with the music of Ives.

[140] Meyer and Shreffler, *Elliott Carter: A Centennial Portrait in Letters and Documents*, 101.

Schmidt, for instance, makes a general observation that the themes and motives in the String Quartet No. 1 appear within a context that is quotational,[141] while Shreffler similarly notes that Carter both quotes a Nancarrow study and devotes much of his music to the "Nancarrow problem": "developing a notation that allows complex rhythmic relationships like those in Rhythm Study No. 1 to be read and performed."[142] Schiff states with a factual tone that "at the beginning of the Variations Carter quotes a passage from Conlon Nancarrow's Study No. 1 as a homage to his polyrhythmic experiments."[143]

However, Nancarrow's theme does not actually appear in Carter's quartet, but rather, the Variations movement, at best, alludes to Nancarrow's *Rhythm Study No. 1*, a piece Carter knew quite well. Carter first heard the piece in January of 1951, when he briefly left the Sonoran Desert to visit Nancarrow in Mexico City. A year later, Carter himself published this etude in *New Music Quarterly*[144] and wrote about Nancarrow's use of "unusual" polyrhythms in *Rhythm Study No. 1*, which employs the combination of four distinct planes of rhythm in the piece's "most elaborate measures" (illustrated in Figure 5).[145]

Figure 5 Conlon Nancarrow, Rhythm Study No. 1, mm. 50–51.

[141] Schmidt, "'I Try to Write Music that Will Appeal to an Intelligent Listener's Ear,'" 174.

[142] Shreffler, "Elliott Carter and His America," 51.

[143] Schiff, *The Music of Elliott Carter*, 70.

[144] *New Music Quarterly* was founded in 1927 by Henry Cowell, who was the journal's editor until 1936, and that was largely supported financially by Charles Ives. The journal was dedicated to the publication of new music, including the scores of Ives, Carl Ruggles, and Nancarrow for the first time. For more information, see R. Mead, *Henry Cowell's New Music, 1925–1936: The Society, the Music Editions, and the Recordings.*

[145] Carter, "The Rhythmic Basis of American Music," 61–62.

Further, sketches for String Quartet No. 1 confirm that Carter was familiar in fine detail with Nancarrow's work while composing his quartet since some of the folios in this collection indicate that he was trying to replicate a part of Nancarrow's rhythmic design. For instance, one sketch shows that Carter is striving to superimpose three polyrhythms in order to create three distinct rhythmic planes.[146] The excerpt is notated in the same tempo and meter as the fourth staff of *Rhythm Study No. 1*: 7/8 meter at the tempo of an eighth note at 210.[147] While the texture and harmony on this sketch show an uncanny resemblance to Nancarrow's score – both are characterized by widely spaced trichords, superimposed fifths in Nancarrow and a combination of fifths and sixths in Carter – this sketch does not make it into the final version of the Quartet. Thus, the sketch suggests that Carter was only using Nancarrow's piece as a study for developing his new rhythmic technique rather than as a direct source of the material; that is, the lack of the actual quotation would imply that the quotation is not literal but, rather, conceptual.

Thus, while the opening of the Variations movement in String Quartet No. 1 *echoes* Nancarrow – it is characterized by four instruments playing themes at distinct speeds, where the top voice plays triple-stops of widely spaced chords and the cello plays accented quarter-note regular downbeats, as illustrated in Figure 6 – the allusion is not a direct quotation as Carter had initially explained it. This mystery is revealed in an unpublished interview Carter conducted in 1982 with Frans van Rossum, in which he explained the context of the missing Nancarrow quotation:

> I first heard some of his piano rolls in 1949/50, when I went to live in Tucson Arizona and we went to visit him in Mexico City and they played some of his new pieces, the first Etude for instance, and [he] then sent me tapes for many years of many of the etudes. Now that they are all coming out on a record, most of these etudes are rather rewritten or repunched. I had quoted in my First String Quartet the opening of the 1st Etude, which in the new version has been changed, so that the quotation is no longer a quotation of the piece that you will hear on the record. I was attracted to this particular part because, and actually the first etude I had published I was [at] that time running Henry Cowell's magazine New Music Edition and we published the score of it and the part that he left out was the part that the work started with[:]

---

[146] See the top three staves of Sketch 0069v in the Elliott Carter Collection, Sketches for String Quartet No. 1 (1951), Library of Congress, www.loc.gov/resource/music.musihas-200155638/?sp=69 (last access July 6, 2024).

[147] For a more detailed analysis of this sketch and Carter's allusion to Nancarrow, see Emmery, "Elliott Carter's First String Quartet: In Search of Proustian Time" and *Compositional Process in Elliott Carter's String Quartets*.

a polyrhythm in a rather slowly beat note in two systems of chords and takes maybe two or three measures to begin, I only quoted this sort of introductory passage which he now cut out because in some ways I suppose it seemed too long and slow. But I found it very dramatic myself. Now he gets into the piece immediately, he cut out I think the first four measures.[148]

The information Carter discloses in this interview is illuminating on two points. First, for Carter scholars, it truly solves the mystery of the missing Nancarrow quotation: simply, it is not there. Second, perhaps even more stunningly, the revelation acknowledges the fact that there was an earlier version of the *Rhythm Study No. 1* with four introductory measures that the composer had cut from his score before its publication. This earlier version of the etude does not survive, as it does not appear within the complete Nancarrow estate housed at the Paul Sacher Stiftung. Thus, in essence, Carter deliberately decided to include a Nancarrow musical quotation and coincidentally Nancarrow happened to cut the said quotation from his piece, ultimately defeating the notion of a musical quotation.

Nevertheless, it is curious that Carter continued to claim, even twenty years later (his essay on his first two string quartets was written in 1970), that the opening of the Variations movement uses a theme from Nancarrow's *Rhythm Study*

Figure 6 Elliott Carter, String Quartet No. 1, Variations, mm. 1–4. Copyright © 1956 (Renewed) by Associated Music Publishers, Inc. International copyright secured. All rights reserved. Used with permission.

---

[148] Frans van Rossum, unpublished interview with Elliott Carter, March 4–6, 1982; typescript sent to Felix Meyer by van Rossum. I would like to thank Felix Meyer for sharing this revealing information with me.

No. 1, even though the theme had been removed from public record. It is even more peculiar that scholars continued to perpetuate this claim when it was evident to everyone who had examined the score that the Nancarrow quotation did not exist. One can only speculate on Carter's intent. What we know for certain is that Carter greatly admired Nancarrow, his music, and especially his rhythmic innovations, and had intended to quote a theme from *Rhythm Study No. 1*. Perhaps, Meyer and Shreffler come closest to finding an explanation – they note that Carter needed to create a narrative of his "open acknowledgment of the American 'ultramodern' tradition of Ives, Ruggles, Cowell, Ruth Crawford Seeger, and Nancarrow" in order to send a clear signal that with his String Quartet No. 1, Carter had left behind neoclassicism and has managed to successfully merge the European traditions" (i.e., Schoenberg, Berg, and Bartók) with the "dissonant" and "advanced" music of the American ultramodernists.[149] Thus, both homages to Ives and Nancarrow were Carter's calculated move to distance himself from *The Minotaur* and *Pocahontas* and create a compelling new narrative of Carter's new, reborn, and modern musical language of String Quartet No. 1.

4 Liège Competition

> I was fortunate in being present at the first European performance of Elliott Carter's quartet when it was presented anonymously in the international competition of 1953 in Liège. Immediately, I and many others felt ourselves in the presence of a truly great work, a work whose complexity and virtually aristocratic indifference to currying favor placed it for us in the company of the last quartets of Beethoven and Bartók.[150]

We see the now-already familiar narrative present in Robert Erich Wolf's 1957 review of Carter's String Quartet No. 1.[151] Wolf's article, published after the performances of the quartet had taken place in both the United States and Rome and around the same time the reviews at home and abroad were being published (including the articles by Rochberg and Goldman), as well as after the release of the recording of the work by Walden Quartet, carries the same language and descriptions established by critics early on: Carter's quartet is discussed in the context of Beethoven and Bartók.[152] However, a close scrutiny of Wolf's review

---

[149] Meyer and Shreffler, *Elliott Carter: A Centennial Portrait in Letters and Documents*, 101.

[150] Wolf, "Review [String Quartet, 1951, by Elliott Carter]," 198.

[151] Wolf, an American scholar studying musicology in Liège, Belgium at the time, attended the 1953 performance of Carter's quartet.

[152] Further, Wolf states that the drama of the quartet "lies in what Mr. Carter calls its 'metrical modulation'" (198). However, Carter did not coin or use that term (although eventually, he adopted it); rather it was Goldman who introduced and defined this term in his 1957 article. However, since Wolf's article was published in March 1957, a month before Goldman's, it would indicate that the two critics discussed Carter's piece amongst themselves.

raises some contention. For instance, it is highly debatable whether the audiences in Liège truly made this assessment on their own; that is, the quartet had already been reviewed in print. But what we do know of this performance in Liège is that the ensemble struggled greatly with Carter's quartet and could barely play it. It is hard to imagine that such a performance would generate such a favorable reception and response from the audience. Even Carter's own recollection of the performance contradicts Wolf's observation:

> When one of the jury was working on the Quartet, they had to have someone conduct it. I don't know how they did it, but they had a terrible time with it. Finally they did play it over the radio, and the only letter I got – this is from Liège, Belgium – was from a Liège coal-miner who said he loved my quartet, just like digging coal [*laughter*].[153]

Joking aside, Wolf's assessment of the grandeur of this performance is highly unlikely – Charles Rosen notes that the players "broke down trying to perform it."[154] In fairness, the committee had received 117 submissions of string quartets in all styles, which the ensemble was supposed to decipher and learn in only two months.[155] Carter's own admission is not only that the performance of his Quartet in Liège was far from great, but that he was utterly surprised when he was notified that he had won the competition. Schiff cites that the reason Carter was surprised is that he felt that sending his piece to Belgium was "like dropping a message-filled bottle off a boat in mid-ocean."[156] This is quite a hyperbolic description of the situation. For one, the Concours international de quatuor à cordes de la ville de Liège [the Liège String Quartet International Competition] was run by the Koussevitzky Music Foundation, an organization with whom Carter had close professional ties. For instance, Carter's *Holiday Overture* (1944) was awarded the first prize at the Independent Music Publishers Contest in 1945; the judges for that contest were Nicolai Berezowsky, Aaron Copland, and Serge Koussevitzky.[157] Thus, Carter submitting his quartet to the Liège competition was not quite like dropping a bottle in the ocean; he knew exactly where it was going and whom it was going to reach.

---

[153] Emmery, "An American Modernist: Teatime with Elliott Carter," 25. For highlights of the reviews following this radio broadcast, see Koch, *Louis Poulet & le concours international de quatuor à cordes de la ville de Liège: Composition–interprétation–lutherie (1951–1972)*, 49–51.

[154] Rosen, "Music and the Cold War."

[155] As this approach was not feasible, the competition organizers reconvened on May 19, 1953 to discuss new measures. They decided to narrow down the selection to eighteen quartets, which would be practiced (on average six hours per day) and recorded through August. On September 7, after listening to the recordings, another elimination process took place behind closed doors (Koch, *Louis Poulet & le concours international de quatuor à cordes de la ville de Liège*, 48).

[156] Schiff, *The Music of Elliott Carter*, 55.

[157] Pascone, "Four Honors Fall to Elliott Carter, Southporters' Son."

Further, Wolf, like Carter himself (and scholars alike), emphasizes and reiterates the point that Carter's submission to the Liège competition was anonymous. This attribute of anonymity is significant as it implies that the work was evaluated objectively and fairly. Even more so, it is a crucial detail because anonymity was one of the criteria of the competition. While Carter did remove his name from the score and entered the competition under the pseudonym Xpovometros (Chronometros, or "timekeeper),"[158] there was, however, nothing anonymous about his submission. That is, one has to wonder: How could it have been possible for Carter to submit his String Quartet No. 1 anonymously, a piece that had already been performed several times by Walden Quartet, had published reviews written about it, and a publication contract in place with American Music Publisher? We may speculate that this is the reason why Carter was actually surprised to learn that he had won the competition: he knew that he was ineligible to compete in the first place, let alone win. The contest rules clearly indicated that the competition was designed for works without prior performances or publications, that the winning piece would be *premiered* by the Liège City String Quartet, and that the organization would arrange the publication of the work. Thus, knowing that Carter had broken the rules of even qualifying for the competition was the truly surprising element of Carter's award.

Carter was in residency at the American Academy in Rome (AAR) in 1953 when he was notified that he had won the Liège competition. Rather than expressing any jubilation, he instead started writing a storm of letters to ensure that he could, indeed, win the award despite his clear ineligibility. He engaged his closest friend, Nicolas Nabokov, Secretary General of the Congress for Cultural Freedom (CCF), who was organizing the 1954 music festival in Rome and programming the Parrenin Quartet's performance of Carter's String Quartet No. 1 in it.[159] Carter strategically reached out to Nabokov to intervene, knowing of his significant political connections and the backing by the United States government. Nabokov attempted to mediate the situation by writing to Louis Poulet, the organizer of the competition and the violist of the Quatuor Municipal de Liège, and proposed that his ensemble participate in the Rome Festival and perform Carter's piece, among others:

> We would like to have the Quatuor Municipal de Liège participate in the concerts, which will take place during the Conference. They will be funded

---

[158] Taruskin, *The Oxford History of Western Music*, vol. 5, ch. 7, § Reception; also see Koch, *Louis Poulet & le concours international de quatuor à cordes de la ville de Liège*, 48.

[159] Carter has known Nabokov since 1933 after attending a concert of his music in Paris and became close friends with him in the early 1940s. In addition to programming his music at festivals, Nabokov also secured Carter his teaching posts at the Peabody Conservatory and St. John's.

by R.A.I., but the programs will be selected by the executive committee for performances.

We would like them to play Elliott Carter's quartet, which won first prize at the Concours de Liège, and to which my friend Paul Collaer tells me, the Quatuor Municipal de Liège has exclusive rights. We have included this quartet on the program for 4 April, but of course we can change the date according to the quartet's availability.[160]

The Liège organizers refused Nabokov's proposal, likely because its quartet could not play Carter's piece. Even during the competition deliberations, Henri Koch wrote in his notes to the jury, "To Chronometros: No! Despite everything! Impossible to play!"[161] Daniel Guberman speculates that Nabokov acted on Carter's request not only out of his wish to help his close friend but likely out of his own (political) interest – he saw an opportunity to expand his Rome Festival by inviting additional European ensembles to perform the works by American composers,[162] thus fulfilling the purpose of the Congress for Cultural Freedom.

But for Carter, winning the Liège competition was primarily about expanding his own international visibility and gaining new professional opportunities. For instance, two days after learning that he was awarded the Liège prize, Carter received a congratulatory letter from Harold Spivacke of the Library of Congress, who was interested in organizing a performance of the work in Washington D.C. and also offered to add Carter's Quartet to the Library of Congress collection.[163] As Guberman speculates, Carter feared that being deemed ineligible for the Liège coemption would result in a significant loss of professional opportunities.[164] Thus, before responding to the Liège competition organizers, Carter sought advice from Olga Koussevitzky of the Koussevitzky Foundation and Richard French of American Music Publisher (asking if AMP would consider collaborating with the City of Liège on the publication of the work),[165] in addition to Nabokov and Spivacke.

---

[160] Guberman, "Victory in Liège? Elliott Carter and the Diplomacy of International Competitions," [15]; a letter from Nicolas Nabokov to Louis Poulet, November 9, 1953, Elliott Carter Collection, Correspondence (Paul Sacher Stiftung). Translated from French by Daniel Guberman.

[161] "Aloha, très bon, personnalité marquante. Pour Xrovometros (Chronometros): Non! Malgré tout! Impossible à jouer!" (Koch, *Louis Poulet & le concours international de quatuor à cordes de la ville de Liège*, 48).

[162] Guberman, "Victory in Liège?" [16].

[163] Guberman, "Composing Freedom: Elliott Carter's 'Self-Reinvention' and the Early Cold War," 153; "Victory in Liège? [5]). Indeed, even though the Paul Sacher Stiftung has secured the right to house the entire Carter collection, the vast majority of the material pertaining to String Quartet No. 1, including sketches, still remains at the Library of Congress.

[164] Guberman, "Composing Freedom," 153; "Victory in Liège?" [6].

[165] Guberman, "Victory in Liège?" [8] and [9].

Eventually, Carter did respond to the Liège competition committee, but as Guberman notes, Carter's letter did not express any "joy, gratitude, or excitement" for winning the award.[166] Instead, he was focusing on the technical wording of the competition regulations and was trying to argue his legality of entering and winning the award. In one letter, Carter writes:

> In submitting the quartet, I felt that I was conforming to Article 3 – "The work should be a manuscript, unpublished and unknown to the public." For although the work had been performed twice in the United States up to that time, it was played in both cases before university audiences, once at Columbia University and once at the University of Illinois in what could be called private performances. Since submitting the score on April 30, 1953, it was performed at an ISCM concert in New York and at a festival in California, always by the Walden Quartet. If, in your opinion, this disqualifies the work, I shall be ready to abide by your decision.[167]

However, the Liège organizers did not succumb to Carter's arguments, notifying him in November 1953, two months after informing him that he had won, that his quartet had been officially disqualified.[168] Nonetheless, Carter (and his supporters) maintained that Carter had won the competition, despite his clear disqualification. Even decades later, Carter still claimed that he did not feel that he had done anything wrong:

> But for my First Quartet, I couldn't accept the Liège prize because the Walden Quartet played it before. I thought they decided not to give it a prize after they have been fooling around with it for over a year, so I didn't feel I was doing anything wrong by having the Walden Quartet play it. So they couldn't give me the prize.[169]

This is, of course, not an accurate portrayal of the events. As Carter himself states in the letter to the Liège competition organizers, the quartet already had two performances in New York before he had even submitted it to the competition, and two additional performances at music festivals since having had submitted it. Further, his argument that university performances should be considered private events is farcical. In a 1952 letter he wrote to John Garvey of the Walden Quartet, upon learning that the ensemble would be performing his

---

[166] Guberman, "Victory in Liège?" [9].

[167] Guberman, "Victory in Liège?" [13]; a letter from Elliott Carter to M. Lecomte, October 21, 1953, Elliott Carter Collection, Correspondence (Paul Sacher Stiftung).

[168] By the time the jury had learned of Carter's ineligibility, it was too late to change the list of winners (Skrowaczewski was initially awarded the second prize, which means that he would have been given the top prize after the reevaluation; Oscar Van Hemel was initially awarded the third prize). The only possible solution was to only sanction Carter by disqualifying his victory (Koch, *Louis Poulet & le concours international de quatuor à cordes de la ville de Liège*, 51).

[169] Emmery, "An American Modernist," 25.

piece at Columbia University, he assured him that he would do his best to secure the attendance of a critic at the concert and be in a position to arrange for the recording of the piece, as well. He writes:

> I have just received an announcement from Columbia University that the Walden Quartet is giving the world premiere of my quartet on Feb. 26. I am delighted indeed and wish to thank you for attacking my difficult work so bravely.
>
> Do you think that your quartet would be interested in making a commercial record of the work at that time? Or would you rather wait? I am quite sure that I can arrange this as there is a recording fund at the ACA. Likewise there is some question of Columbia Records doing some music of mine on the chamber music series and perhaps this tie up could be made.
>
> I will do what I can to get a reasonable critic to come to this concert, but, as you realise this particular series is seldom covered by the press.[170]

Clearly, Carter was not envisioning a private event but rather a public premiere that would be covered by the press and result in a recording of the work. This is precisely why Carter, upon learning that he had been awarded the Liège prize, instead of celebrating his achievement, sought advice from his friends on how he could bypass his ineligibility due to prior public performances of his quartet and keep the prize. But the question arises: Why did such a small, and rather insignificant competition that hardly anyone had really heard of before Carter, matter so much to him?

The Concours international de quatuor à cordes de la ville de Liège was founded in 1951 by Louis Poulet, a violist of the Liège City String Quartet[171] and a professor of chamber music at the Royal Conservatory of Music in Brussels, and Paul Renotte, a councilman of fine arts in the city of Liège. It was sponsored by the Koussevitzky Music Foundation and in addition to the members of its Foundation, the committee comprised Fernand Quinet (president of the jury), Paul Collaer (Belgian musicologist, pianist, and orchestra director), Léon Jongen (a composer and pianist), Henri Koch and Éric Feldbusch (members of the string quartet), Marcel Deprez, and Poulet.[172] The competition, focused solely on the genre of the string quartet, was designed with a three-part structural objective in mind, which would undoubtedly result in making Liège "the string quartet capital of the world": emphasizing composition through its string quartet competition; focusing on the performance by hosting workshops and inviting quartet ensembles to play the new literature submitted to the competition; and highlighting instrument-making, which

---

[170] Guberman, "Composing Freedom," 151; Elliott Carter to John Garvey, October 10, 1952, Elliott Carter Collection, Correspondence (Paul Sacher Stiftung).

[171] Other members of the Quartet were Henri Koch (first violin), Emmanuel Koch (second violin), and Éric Feldbush (cello).

[172] Koch, *Louis Poulet & le concours international de quatuor à cordes de la ville de Liège*, 47–48.

awarded new instruments to the winners of the competition.[173] The competition ran for only twenty years, from 1951 through 1971, and the three components of the competition – composition, performance, and instrument-making – alternated each September. Thus, within those twenty years, the composition competition sessions occurred only eight times: in 1951, 1953, 1956, 1962, 1965, 1969, and 1972.[174] Out of those eight events, the first prize was awarded only five times, including Carter's 1953 award, which was subsequently withdrawn. Therefore, there have been a total of four prizes awarded successfully during the competition's short-lived history: to a Polish composer, Grażyna Bacewicz, in 1951; French composer, Manfred Kelkel, in 1956; Italian composer, Giorgio Ferrari, in 1962; and a Romanian composer, Wilhelm Georg Berger, in 1965.[175] The documents also show a significant decrease in the number of submissions following the competition's early excitement: in 1953, there were 117 submissions and by 1959 only 25.[176] Thus, one may conclude that the Liège string quartet competition was hardly a success story or that it had a big impact on the new music scene. Perhaps, the most notable detail concerning the Liège competition is that in 1953, Carter beat Stanisław Skrowaczewski, who was awarded the second prize.[177] Carter's victory in Liège, and we can certainly call it that despite his disqualification for there is hardly a discussion of Carter's String Quartet No. 1 without a mention of the Liège competition,[178] did not put him on a musical map; rather, Carter's victory put Liège on the map.

To return to the initial question – why was Carter intent on keeping the prize of a rather insignificant competition? It was likely about the prestige of winning an international prize, which would ensure Carter greater visibility. Also, Carter likely bought into the optimism shared by the organizers and sponsors in Liège that the competition would become an up-and-coming event; with 117 submissions in 1953, it did gain some notice in Europe and the United States, thus the notion of Liège becoming "the string quartet capital of the world," while naïve, may have seemed momentarily plausible.[179] But, for Carter, it was also about winning a prize for a piece that featured his new compositional ideas and would thus justify the composer's drastic shift in his musical expression. Even though Carter had won some accolades before Liège – his *Pocahontas* was awarded the Juilliard Publication Award in 1940 and *Holiday Overture* the Independent Music

---

[173] Koch, *Louis Poulet & le concours international de quatuor à cordes de la ville de Liège.*

[174] Koch, *Louis Poulet & le concours international de quatuor à cordes de la ville de Liège.*

[175] Koch, *Louis Poulet & le concours international de quatuor à cordes de la ville de Liège.* During the 1959, 1969, and the last competition in 1972, the jury did not award the first prize.

[176] Koch, *Louis Poulet & le concours international de quatuor à cordes de la ville de Liège,* 48.

[177] Koch, *Louis Poulet & le concours international de quatuor à cordes de la ville de Liège,* 50.

[178] For instance, see Emmery, *Compositional Process in Elliott Carter's String Quartets*; Schiff, *The Music of Elliott Carter*; and Rao, "*Allegro scorrevole* in Carter's First String Quartet."

[179] I would like to thank the anonymous reviewer for this insight.

Publishers Contest in 1945 – those were recognitions for his old-fashioned, neoclassical compositions. His String Quartet No. 1 was a direct statement on Carter distancing himself from the populist compositional trend; winning an award for his new, modern, and "advanced" composition would warrant him the necessary validation from critics, performers, and audiences.

Naturally, the notion of winning in itself also carried certain pride and appeal for Carter. For instance, while discussing his *Holiday Overture* at a lecture in 1965, Carter could not help but mention that he was awarded the first prize at the Music Publishers Contest over Schoenberg:

> My music is always written directly for the orchestra. Most of it can't be played on the piano. I remember when I wrote this piece [*Holiday Overture*] back in 1944, I made a piano reduction of it and tried to play it with Aaron Copland for piano four-hands. We made such a mess of it that I went home and decided that the whole piece was a mistake. [*Laughter.*] It was submitted to a prize contest and, to my surprise, it won a prize. To my embarrassment, a number of years later I discovered that one of the other contestants was Arnold Schoenberg. [*Laughter.*] He must have felt very badly about it. I never found out what the piece was that he had submitted. I am glad I never did.[180]

Making light of the situation, Carter reveals not only that he had beaten Schoenberg in a composition contest, but that he did so with a piece he had just ridiculed. Thus, we can assume that if even winning a competition with a mediocre piece brought Carter certain validation, then winning a competition with a "serious" composition would carry much more weight. Thus, for Carter, this is why winning in Liège mattered, even though ultimately, he did not win the award following his disqualification – it was about his reputation, visibility, and confirmation. However, for the Koussevitzky Music Foundation, Nicolas Nabokov, the Congress for Cultural Freedom, and the United States government, Carter's victory mattered in the context of politics and cultural diplomacy of the Cold War.

5 Political Ideals of Individualism and Freedom

On February 14, 1967, the *New York Times* published a front-page story in which the reporter, Neil Sheehan, uncovered that the Central Intelligence Agency (CIA) had been secretly supporting the nation's largest student organization – the National Student Organization (Figure 7).[181] In the weeks that followed,

---

[180] Emmery, *Elliott Carter Speaks*, 118.
[181] Sheehan, "A Student Group Concedes It Took Funds from C.I.A.," 1, 7.

The New York Times.

"All the News That's Fit to Print"

LATE CITY EDITION
U.S. Weather Bureau Report (Page 25) Forecast:
Partly cloudy, milder today; fair tonight, partly cloudy tomorrow.
Temp. Range: 42—23; yesterday: 23—4.

VOL. CXVI...No. 39,833.   © 1967 by The New York Times Company. Times Square, New York, N. Y. 10036.   NEW YORK, TUESDAY, FEBRUARY 14, 1967.   10 CENTS

A STUDENT GROUP CONCEDES IT TOOK FUNDS FROM C.I.A.

National Association Says It Received Aid From Early 1950's Until Last Year

ROLE IN SPYING DENIED

Leader Asserts All Money Was Used to Help Pay for Overt Activities Abroad

By NEIL SHEEHAN
Special to The New York Times

WASHINGTON, Feb. 13—The National Student Association, the largest college student organization in the country, conceded today that it received funds from the Central Intelligence Agency from the early nineteen-fifties until last year.

Eugene Groves, president of the association, said the C.I.A. funds had been used to help finance the association's international activities, including sending representatives to student congresses abroad and funding student exchange programs.

The intelligence agency refused tonight to comment on the matter.

The association has chapters on more than 300 American college and university campuses, where about 1.5 million students are studying. The local student government organizations rather than the individual students themselves form the membership.

FOUND IN LIBRARY: Two pages from manuscript by Leonardo da Vinci show variety of his inventions. At right are links and chain drives, much like those on bicycles.

Escapement, upper left, is used to convert linear into rotary motion as plunger is pushed down. At left center are two simple release mechanisms, like those in cranes.

700 Pages of Leonardo MSS. Found in Madrid

By WALTER SULLIVAN
Special to The New York Times

BOSTON, Feb. 13 — Some 700 pages of manuscript and drawings by Leonardo da Vinci, lost for almost two centuries, have been found in the National Library in Madrid.

The drawings, most of them done near the end of the 15th century, are said to establish

chain drive familiar to all bicycle riders.

They increase by a substantial amount the surviving fruits of Leonardo's genius. About 5,000 pages of his manuscript material were hitherto available. The added 700 pages contain some of his most elaborate and careful drawings.

was the wont of the "great doodler," whose output during the period when he wrote these documents included also his famous fresco, "The Last Supper," in a monastery in Milan.

The finding was announced today jointly by two scholars, Dr. Jules Piccus, who made the discovery accidentally

authenticated the documents two weeks ago.

Dr. Piccus is a professor of Romance languages at the University of Massachusetts in Amherst. He was searching the library at Madrid for popular ballads of the medieval period when he noticed a gap in the numerical sequence of catalogue cards.

U.S. RENEWS RAIDS IN NORTH, BUT PLEDGES PEACE EFFORT, AS DO MOSCOW AND LONDON

SOVIET SHIFT SEEN

Kosygin Ends British Visit With Pledge to Seek Halt in War

Text of London communiqué is printed on Page 10.

By ANTHONY LEWIS
Special to The New York Times

LONDON, Feb. 13—The Soviet Union and Britain pledged today to "make every possible effort" for peace in Vietnam and agreed to "maintain contact to this end."

This modest language was regarded by the British as signifying a shift in Soviet policy—toward a willingness to speak out and work for an end to the fighting in Vietnam. The British feeling is that the Russians urgently want the conflict to stop.

In a communiqué issued at the end of Premier Aleksei N. Kosygin's seven-day visit here, the British and Soviet Governments also announced that they would install a hot line similar to the one between Moscow and Washington. It will connect teleprinters in the Kremlin and 10 Downing Street.

Ho Chi Minh Asks Pope to Press U.S.

The text of message to Pope will be found on Page 8.

Special to The New York Times

HONG KONG, Feb. 13 — President Ho Chi Minh of North Vietnam called on Pope Paul VI today to urge the United States to "respect the national rights of the Vietnamese people."

The message, which was broadcast by the Hanoi radio, was in reply to the Pope's plea of Feb. 8 for action to transform the lunar new year cease-fire into negotiations for "a just and stable peace." The reply was made public before the United States resumed raids on the North.

Observers here said that while President Ho Chi Minh placed on the United States the responsibility of bringing about conditions for a settlement, his message was a more encouraging response than any previous reaction by

Continued on Page 8, Column 1

JUSTICES REJECT DRAFT TEST CASE

JOHNSON EXPLAINS

Says Foe Used Pause to Send Supplies to Troops in South

By JOHN W. FINNEY
Special to The New York Times

WASHINGTON, Feb. 13—The United States resumed the bombing of North Vietnam today after a pause of nearly six days.

In explaining his decision to resume the attacks, President Johnson said the United States had "no alternative but to resume full-scale hostilities" in view of the use of the truce by the North Vietnamese for "major resupply efforts of their troops in South Vietnam" rather than to seek a peaceful settlement of the war.

The President emphasized, however, that "the door is open and will remain open" to a negotiated settlement.

The President's statement was issued about four hours after the bombing was resumed at 12:07 P.M. Eastern standard time (1:07 A.M. Tuesday, Saigon time) with strikes against targets in the southern section of North Vietnam.

Figure 7 *New York Times*, February 14, 1967 front-page report uncovering the CIA secret operations. Used with permission.

the *New York Times* continued to publish a series of articles further exposing the CIA's infiltration and financial support of journalists, academics, intellectuals, book and journal publishers, and arts organizations, all of whom were engaged in the diffusion of the Cold War propaganda at the height of the Cold War. Among them, notably stood out a British American magazine *Encounter* (which published an overtly glowing review of Carter's Quartet by Glock in 1954, following the performance in Rome). Together with *Encounter*, which in 1953 became the official voice of the Congress for Cultural Freedom, the CCF itself was also identified as a beneficiary of the CIA's secret funding. Frances Stonor Saunders claims that the CCF received around one million dollars per year in the early 1960s via the Ford Foundation to organize music festivals in Europe and run several magazines, including *Encounter.*[182]

The *New York Times* exposé created a scandal for the CIA, all of the foundations engaged with its secret plan, and the individuals who accepted its money.[183] The US Congress urged an investigation and President Lyndon B. Johnson ordered the CIA to immediately cease all its secret funding of student groups.[184] The scandal reached its apex on May 8, 1967, when Tom Braden, the former chief of the CIA's International Organization Division, confirmed that "the C.I.A. 'placed' an 'agent' in the Congress for Cultural Freedom, an organization of leading European and American intellectuals," and that "'another agent became an editor of *Encounter*,' a London-based intellectual monthly once supported by the [CCF]."[185] Braden further explained that these "agents" suggested programs and projects to the CIA and arranged for agency subsidies that were channeled through real or fake

---

[182] See Saunders, *Who Paid the Piper? The Cultural Cold War: The CIA and the World of Arts and Letters.*

[183] Interestingly, historian Tity de Vries notes that the newspapers had previously reported about the CIA's secret financing of private foundations, following the 1964 congressional investigation of the tax-exempt status of certain foundations, which found that eight of them served as umbrella organizations for the CIA. De Vries further points to the September 14, 1964 editorial in the *Nation*, which questioned whether the CIA could be "permitted to channel funds to magazines in London – and New York – which pose as 'magazines of opinion' and are in competition with independent journals of opinion" and whether it was a "legitimate function" of the CIA "to finance, indirectly, various congresses, conventions, assemblies and conferences devoted to cultural freedom' and kindred topics" (originally in the *Nation* Editorial, "Foundations as 'Fronts,'" 102–3; quoted in de Vries, "The 1967 Central Intelligence Agency Scandal: Catalyst in a Transforming Relationship between State and People," 1078; also see Saunders, *Who Paid the Piper?*, 354; Wilford, *The Mighty Wurlitzer: How the CIA Played America*). Yet, these early articles caused some stir in the United States, but not an outrage. De Vries posits that the reason that the 1967 revelations of the same stories caused such a scandal is because the political climate had drastically changed in 1967; that is, there was an increasingly growing unpopularity and opposition to the Vietnam War, which led the media to be more critical in its coverage of the government policy and government agencies, such as the CIA.

[184] de Vries, "The 1967 Central Intelligence Agency Scandal," 1076.

[185] Frankel, "Ex-Official of C.I.A. Lists Big Grants to Labor Aides," 36.

foundations.[186] Another article on the same *New York Times* front page reported that Stephen Spender, a British poet and a co-editor of *Encounter*, left his post following the disclosure of the CIA's role with the journal (Figure 8).[187] A week later, on May 13, 1967, during a board meeting of the CCF, Michael Josselson, the executive director of the organization and a CIA agent, resigned after admitting that he had been misleading the CCF for twenty years with obscured facts and that the CCF was part of a secret CIA operation.[188] Following these revelations, the Congress for Cultural Freedom continued to operate for about a decade under a new name, the International Association for Cultural Freedom. But, with an irreparably damaged reputation, it failed to gain any prominence or support, and the Congress fully dissolved in 1979.[189]

With the backing and financial support of the CIA and the American military government, the Congress for Cultural Freedom was initiated in West Berlin in 1950 (June 26–29) during a conference of more than one hundred American and European intellectuals, who espoused a notion that "culture can exist only in freedom and that freedom can lead to cultural progress."[190] The key figures at this meeting and the subsequent formation of the CCF were Melvin Lasky (1920–2004), an American trade unionist serving as a cultural attaché with the Army of Occupation and founder of its German-language monthly *Der Monat*, who would soon become a co-editor of *Encounter*; Michael Josselson (1908–1978), a Jewish immigrant from Estonia, a former member of the Army's Psychological Warfare Division, who had left the US army to work for the CIA; and Nicolas Nabokov (1903–1978), a Russian-born composer and writer, and a cousin of Vladimir Nabokov, who after exiling Russia became the director of Russian broadcasts of Voice for America and was later appointed CCF's Secretary General.

Headquartered in Paris, the CCF was successfully spreading its mission across the globe, establishing chapters in 35 countries within the first ten years of its operation. As Tity de Vries argues, the CCF was the "cultural counterpart to the North Atlantic Treaty Organization," because it was considered one of the most important organizations with which the United States

---

[186] Frankel, "Ex-Official of C.I.A. Lists Big Grants to Labor Aides," 36.

[187] Fox, "Stephen Spender Quits Encounter: British Poet Says Finding of C.I.A. Financing Led to His Leaving Magazine," 1, 37.

[188] de Vries, "The 1967 Central Intelligence Agency Scandal," 1088.

[189] de Vries, "The 1967 Central Intelligence Agency Scandal," 1088.

[190] Quoted in de Vries, "The 1967 Central Intelligence Agency Scandal," 1079. For more on the history of the formation of the CCF, see Harris, *The CIA and the Congress for Cultural Freedom in the Early Cold War: The Limits of Making Common Sense*, and Scott-Smith, *The Politics of Apolitical Culture: The Congress for Cultural Freedom and the Political Economy of American Hegemony 1945–1955*.

Figure 8 *New York Times*, May 8, 1967, front-page headlines covering the CIA scandal. Used with permission.

conducted its "cultural Cold War."[191] That is, economically, the United States came out on top after the Second World War. However, ideologically, it was still fighting the spread of communism in Western Europe and Asia, especially encountering challenges in countries like France and Italy, where the doctrine was gaining popularity. Thus, the US government was looking for ways to squash the support and sympathy of the communist ideology by winning the "hearts and minds" of the people in nonaligned countries, as Hugh Wilford notes. Hence, the CIA envisioned an organization that would enlist artists and intellectuals, among others, to actively engage in spreading their message of cultural freedom across the world.[192] The organization's mission was to subsidize dozens of prominent magazines, hold music festivals, art exhibits, and international conferences on themes such as "science and freedom" and "the end of ideology," which, as de Vries states, was guaranteed to attract the most notable speakers among Western intellectuals.[193] Thus, at one of the secret meetings in London in 1951, the CIA and the UK's Secret Intelligence Service, MI6, convened to discuss the idea of forming an "Anglo-American left-of-center" publication, which led to the founding of *Encounter*. While the editors were "free to publish anything they wanted," the articles were expected "not to adversely affect American interest."[194] That is, financed and handled mostly by the CIA, the *Encounter* operated on the guidance of the CIA.[195] In order to successfully execute this operation (dubbed QKOPERA), the CIA formed an alliance with "largely Jewish ex-Communists," who had not only severed their relations with Moscow but had become "virulently anti-Communist." Once the relationships were established, the CIA secretly funneled money out of the Marshall Plan[196] into the hands of these individuals, either through the creation of fake philanthropies or through existing ones, such as the Ford Foundation and the CCF.[197]

There is no consensus among scholars on how successful the CIA really was in influencing the CCF, especially concerning the kind of music being programmed in its festivals. For instance, Saunders and Joel Whitney argue that the CIA had complete control over Congress in promoting "cutting edge" modernism and that the CCF's many participants, either willingly or unknowingly, had successfully

---

[191] de Vries, "The 1967 Central Intelligence Agency Scandal," 1079.

[192] See Wilford, *The Mighty Wurlitzer: How the CIA Played America*, 5–6.

[193] de Vries, "The 1967 Central Intelligence Agency Scandal," 1079.

[194] Saunders, "How the CIA Plotted against Us"; also see *Who Paid the Piper?*, 165–89.

[195] Saunders, "How the CIA Plotted against Us"; also see *Who Paid the Piper?*, 165–89.

[196] The Marshall Plan was established in 1948 to help rebuild Western Europe following the devastation caused by the Second World War. Congress passed the plan and allotted $12 billion to the program. See Office of the Historian, "Marshall Plan, 1948."

[197] Zuckerman, "How the C.I.A. Played Dirty Tricks with Culture."

manipulated the Cold War culture to the detriment of the global left by actively engaging in propagating the pro-American and anti-Communist ideas. As Patrick Iber surmises, these scholars "understand the CIA as an instrument of the United States ruling class and the CCF as its representative on the international intellectual field."[198] Taruskin more explicitly suggests that there was an ideological connection between cultural freedom and specifically the avant-garde and serialism.[199] However, other scholars question the actual impact of the CIA, arguing that the agency had no preference for promoting modern music; they also point to the individuals who resisted the US government's demands, as Carter had. For instance, Greg Barnhisel, in his *Cold War Modernists*, without disputing the CCF's "hegemonic intentions," as Iber notes, found relatively little editorial interference by the CCF in the operations of its flagship English-language journal *Encounter*.[200] Similarly, Hugh Wilford in his *The Mighty Wurlitzer* argues that even when the CIA tried to "call the tune," it did not always get what it wanted,[201] while Ian Wellens, in his close study of Nabokov and his role in the CCF, concludes that there is no evidence to support the notion that the goal of the CCF was to promote atonal and modern works.[202] Even more bluntly, Charles Rosen, stated that "there is no evidence at all that the CIA was interested in twelve-tone music or even simply in difficult and dissonant modernism."[203] As his proof, Rosen points to the CCF 1954 Rome Music Festival program organized by Nabokov. However, Taruskin accused Rosen of his blind support for Elliott Carter and aptly notes that both Rosen and Carter have been "beneficiaries" of the Cold War "prestige machine" in which they were "willing participants."[204] Carter was particularly well-positioned within this "machinery" – Nabokov was championing Carter's music through rigorous programming of his works at international festivals, while Glock was writing favorable reviews in *Encounter*, all through the backing of the CCF, sponsored by the CIA.

In 1953–54, Elliott Carter (together with Yehudi Wyner) was selected as a fellow of the American Academy in Rome (AAR). As a Secretary General of

---

[198] Iber, "The Spy Who Funded Me: Revisiting the Congress for Cultural Freedom." In *Neither Peace nor Freedom: The Cultural Cold War in Latin America*, Iber argues that the CCF produced unexpected and contradictory effects in Latin America in its pursuit of intellectual hegemony, such as when it helped Fidel Castro come to power in Cuba.

[199] See Taruskin, *The Oxford History of Western Music*, vol. 5, "Standoff (II)," 293.

[200] Barnhisel, *Cold War Modernists: Art, Literature, and American Cultural Diplomacy*; also see Iber, *Neither Peace nor Freedom*.

[201] Wilford, *The Mighty Wurlitzer*.

[202] Wellens, *Music on the Frontline: Nicolas Nabokov's Struggle against Communism and Middlebrow Culture*.

[203] Rosen, "Music and the Cold War." Rosen is responding to Taruskin, "Afterword: Nicht blutbefleckt?"

[204] Taruskin, *The Oxford History of Western Music*, vol. 5, ch. 6, § At the Pinnacle.

the CCF and a composer in residence that year at the AAR, Nicolas Nabokov organized a festival, "Music of the XX Century" [La Musica nel XX° Secolo]. In addition to the concert, the ten-day festival also featured six discussions, thirteen concerts, two operas, and a composition competition.[205] That the festival was sponsored by several prominent corporations and foundations, such as the European Centre of Culture of Geneva, Italian radio-television (RAI), the Rockefeller Foundation, and various offices of several NATO countries,[206] speaks of Nabokov's influence, reach, and power. And that the event was considered a crucial cultural diplomatic event is evident from the fact that the US government, other than financing the festival through the CCF, also sent Samuel Barber, Aaron Copland, Leonard Bernstein, and Virgil Thomson to join Carter, Wyner, and Nabokov at the Academy.[207] Wyner, in a conversation with Martin Brody, vividly describes how surreal the event was, with the attendance of the most prominent artists and intellectuals, and thus illustrating how well-connected and vital Nabokov was during this period:

> I don't know if Nicolas organized the party, but a lot of his famous friends were there. [...] I especially remember seeing Poulenc, slouched in a low chair with his head in his hands [...] I assumed that he was ashamed to be in the presence of Stravinsky. [...] I walked up to [Stravinsky] and said something inane about what an honor it was to meeting him. [...] Then I was introduced to Salvador Dali. [...]
>
> As for the Italian literati, I didn't know those people; that was Elliott's crowd. I don't know if [Ignazio] Silone was there, but he was a close friend of Elliott.
>
> Sam Barber and Lenny and Aaron and some others had come to Rome, but I don't remember if they were at the party.[208]

The music programmed at the Rome Festival led scholars like Taruskin and Saunders to conclude that the CCF was particularly promoting avant-garde music as an effective tool to spread its message of artistic freedom, which stood in direct opposition to the restrictions imposed by the Soviet doctrine of socialist realism. Taruskin, for instance, suggests that the purpose of the festival was to "nominate, through showcase concerts and a series of prize competitions, a corps of standard-bearers for the Congress's highly politicized notion of cultural freedom, which in reality boiled down to sponsorship of the avant-garde, the type of art most obviously uncongenial to totalitarian taste."[209] Similarly, Saunders surmises that "with a heavy concentration on atonal,

---

[205] Brody, "Class of '54: Friendship and Ideology at the American Academy in Rome," 233.
[206] Brody, "Class of '54," 233.
[207] Brody, "Class of '54," 233.
[208] Brody, "Class of '54," 232–33.
[209] Taruskin, *The Oxford History of Western Music*, vol. 5, "Standoff (II)," 293.

dodecaphonic compositions, the aesthetic direction of the event pointed very much to the progressive avant-garde of Alban Berg, Elliott Carter, Luigi Dallapiccola and Luigi Nono." She continues, "amongst the 'new' composers were Peter Racine Fricker, Lou Harrison and Mario Peragallo, whose works were influenced in varying degrees by twelve-tone composition. [...] A recent convert to twelve-tone music was Stravinsky."[210] However, Saunders conveniently leaves out a majority of composers programmed at the Rome Festival, whose music was a direct denunciation of the "progressive avant-garde": Samuel Barber, Francis Poulenc, Ralph Vaughan Williams, Benjamin Britten, Darius Milhaud, Erik Satie, Dmitri Shostakovich, and Sergei Prokofiev, among many others.[211] One could easily argue that the music program at the 1954 Rome Festival was predominantly traditional, in comparison to a handful of "progressive," "avant-garde," or "serial" composers. For instance, Joseph Straus's empirical study on the prevalence of serial and atonal music in North America in the 1950s and 1960s, which in part relied on his statistical analysis of concert programs during this period, confirms that these compositions were in the minority of programmed works.[212] Further, as Wellens notes, it would have been impossible and unrealistic to avoid serialist compositions at *any* music festival in the 1950s,[213] as the trend was gaining popularity at US academic institutions and Darmstadt. Thus, by numbers, as Straus's study would confirm, the Rome Festival program did not look any more progressive or "serialist" than any other new music event. However, as Shreffler points out in her critical response to Straus's attempt at empirical historiography, although serial and atonal works may have been programmed more scarcely, their impact was, nonetheless, enormous.[214]

But, a position that all scholars can easily agree on is that Carter had much to gain from his friendship with Nabokov and by having his String Quartet No. 1 programmed at the Rome Festival. For one, Nabokov, Aaron Copland, and Walter Piston (Carter's former composition teacher at Harvard) were on the Rome Prize selection committee the year Carter was awarded the fellowship.[215]

---

[210] Saunders, *Who Paid the Piper?*, 135–36.

[211] Taruskin argues that the inclusion of Shostakovich and Prokofiev was political, in that their music was programmed to embarrass the Soviets: while their major works were under a post-Zhdanov ban in their own country, in Rome they were promoted as masterpieces and received high acclaim (*The Oxford History of Western Music*, vol. 5, ch. 7, § Reception).

[212] See Straus, "The Myth of Serial 'Tyranny' in the 1950s and 1960s." However, in her critical response to Straus's "simplification" of the matter, Shreffler argues that a shift about the ways of thinking about music most certainly took place after 1945 and even though these works may have been programmed more scarcely, their impact was, nonetheless, enormous; see Shreffler, "The Myth of Empirical Historiography: A Response to Joseph N. Straus."

[213] Wellens, *Music on the Frontline*, 121.

[214] See Shreffler, "The Myth of Empirical Historiography: A Response to Joseph N. Straus."

[215] See Wierzbicki, *Elliott Carter*, 51.

James Wierzbicki proposes that whether or not Carter's success can be attributed to Nabokov's influence, the documentary evidence shows that "the performance of Carter's Frist String Quartet in the 1954 Rome Festival did require Nabokov to pull strings." He further explains that "the correspondence between Nabokov, Fred Goldbeck (an administrator for the FCC), and the Parrenin Quartet indicated that Carter's Quartet would not have been performed in Rome without Nabokov's intervention,"[216] because the Paris-based Parrenin Quartet, one of the most prestigious ensembles specializing in contemporary music at the time, found Carter's quartet *"trop difficile"* – that is, impossible to play. Instead, a piece by Hans Werner Henze was proposed as an alternate.[217]

Even though the performance of Carter's Quartet in Rome received mixed reviews from the critics, as noted earlier, both Carter and his quartet became an international hit. He gained a following and admiration among prominent Italian figures, including Enzo Restagno, Roman Vlad, Goffredo Petrassi, and Dallapiccola. However, I would argue that no other person contributed more to Carter's success than Nicolas Nabokov, a man at the center of the American cultural Cold War. After all, Carter's String Quartet No. 1 received a rather modest reception in the United States following the performances by the Walden Quartet. However, in Europe, the piece was a much bigger success, entirely thanks to Nabokov's efforts. That is, after appointing Carter as a fellow at the Academy in Rome and fighting hard to keep Carter's quartet at the festival in Rome, Nabokov programmed and promoted Carter's quartet (and later his other pieces) at numerous festivals in Europe and Asia, including the performance of String Quartet No. 1 at the United States Information Service in Paris in 1957 and Warsaw Festival in 1960, the Cello Sonata at the Begegnungen Festival in Berlin in 1963, and String Quartet No. 2 at the East-West Festival in Tokyo in 1961.

In addition to Nabokov's direct involvement in championing Carter's music, he also introduced Carter to many prominent figures during his residency in Rome and helped him nurture those relationships, which would prove vital. For instance, in 1955, Goffredo Petrassi was elected international president of the International Society for Contemporary Music (ISCM), while Carter and Vlad were its vice presidents. Under Petrassi's leadership, Carter enjoyed quite a few performances of his music, mostly in Italy. Further, Laurance Roberts, who was director of the AAR during Carter's fellowship, appointed Carter three times as a composer in residence at the Academy – in 1963, 1969, and 1980. William Glock, who in 1959 became BBC Controller of Music, arranged for numerous

---

[216] Wierzbicki, *Elliott Carter*, 51.

[217] Also see Brody, "Cold War Genius: Music and Cultural Diplomacy at the American Academy in Rome."

broadcasts of Carter's music, wrote supportive reviews, and in 1957 invited Carter to teach at the Dartington International Summer School (UK), which he founded in 1953, and also programmed Carter's pieces in its festivals. Mario Labroca, who was director of the music program at the RAI during Carter's residency in Rome, arranged performance series of AAR fellows by the RAI orchestra. Labroca later became the organizer of the Venice Biennale, where Carter's String Quartet No. 2 was performed in 1960. Labroca became the president of the UNESCO International Music Council in 1959. Carter's String Quartet No. 2 (composed in 1959) was awarded the first prize at the UNESCO competition a year later (in 1960).

Akin to Taruskin's view, most of Carter's accomplishments and prestige (if not all) were achieved as a consequence of Nabokov's efforts (i.e., also by the CIA and the US State Department, by extension) to combat the Soviet propaganda during the Cold War. Even though Carter's String Quartet No. 1 received much greater success in Europe, after his return to the United States, Carter enjoyed a boost in demand for his participation in various festivals and lectureships.[218] For instance, Carter was appointed inaugural composer in a Ford Foundation Fellowship program in Berlin, once again with help from Nabokov, who was an advisor to the Foundation's Berlin program. By 1960, Carter established himself as one of the most esteemed American composers, having won the Pulitzer Prize for Music for his String Quartet No. 2.[219]

Carter's knowledge of the extent of the US State Department's and CIA's cultural cold war is perhaps somewhat debatable. While it would be naive to think that he was unaware of Nabokov's connections and what that meant for his own achievements – after all, he did reach out to his friend for help in sorting out the trouble in Liège – the documents show that Carter was a participant in the government's diplomatic plans willingly and only when it suited him in the advancement of his career. Unlike Aaron Copland, who between the 1940s and the 1980s served as one of the most dedicated cultural ambassadors for the State Department and, as Emily Abrams Ansari observes, was truly concerned with helping the United States build peaceful relationships with other nations,[220] Carter was less diplomatic in his affairs with the government. For instance, following his surprising success in Liège, the US State Department offered Carter a one-year Fulbright residency in Belgium, hoping that Carter would stay and promote the ideals of American freedom that enabled him to pursue new

---

[218] For instance, most notable among his lecture series are the Dartmouth lectures from 1963, preserved as audio recordings, housed at the Paul Sacher Stiftung, and the 1967 Minnesota lectures, transcribed, edited, and published by Emmery, *Elliott Carter Speaks*.

[219] Carter won another Pulitzer Prize for Music in 1973 for his Third String Quartet (1971).

[220] See Ansari, "Aaron Copland and the Politics of Cultural Diplomacy."

ideas and compose complex modern music, as exemplified in his String Quartet
No. 1. However, Carter refused their offer, citing that he would, personally, have
very little to gain by living in Belgium for a year:

> As to your suggestion about my lecturing in Brussels next year – while
> I understand that my winning the Liège prize for my string quartet the
> performances of which caused a great deal of interest, I do not think that
> my lectures on American music would be of very great interest in Belgium.
> Besides this, quite selfishly, I wish to live in an important musical center
> next year if I stay in Europe, for in that way I can get performances of
> American music not well known to Europeans, and can learn what is being
> done on this continent. I feel that Brussels has very little to offer in this way,
> and for this reason I do not wish to take up your suggestion.[221]

Carter's lack of diplomatic skills is understandable. As Danielle Fosler-Lussier
points out, the musicians who served as the State Department cultural ambassadors were not trained diplomats and were seldom sufficiently briefed or trained
about diplomacy or politics before their trips abroad, topics in which they
tended to have little interest. Fosler-Lussier thus concludes that given their
"lack of concern with the political aspects of their mission," these touring
musicians "made unlikely diplomats."[222]

After Carter failed to persuade the State Department to grant him a Fulbright
fellowship in Paris, London, or Munich instead, or as he noted in the same letter –
"in an important musical center" – he returned to the United States in 1954, after
only one year of residency in Rome. Four years later, an independently wealthy
Carter reached out to the State Department directly to inquire about the possibility
of financial support for his trip to Poland. Four years later, in 1958 Carter was
invited to participate as an observer in the Warsaw Autumn Festival. However,
Carter found himself once again at odds with the government in his attempt at
cultural diplomacy after learning that the US government did not financially
support activities in Poland and thus would not support his trip.[223] Consequently,
Carter did not attend the festival.[224]

In 1959, the US State Department reached out to Carter once again. This time,
they were inviting him on a two-month tour of the Soviet Union and Eastern
Europe as part of a newly established cultural exchange program, initiated by
Nikita Khrushchev, between the US and USSR. That is, in 1958, the two countries

---

[221] Elliott Carter to Francis A. Young, March 13, 1954, Elliott Carter Collection, Correspondence
(Paul Sacher Stiftung).

[222] Fosler-Lussier, *Music in America's Cold War Diplomacy*, 33–34.

[223] Guberman, "Composing Freedom," 174.

[224] However, by 1962, as evident from his "Letter from Europe," Carter did attend the Warsaw
Autumn – the most elaborate of annual festivals" – and even arranged to provide the festival's
music directors with scores by American composers (37–38).

signed an "Agreement ... on Exchanges in the Cultural, Technical, and Educational Fields."[225] In its first tour, the US government sent Roy Harris, Ulysses Kay, Peter Mennin, and Roger Sessions.[226] In 1959, the Soviet delegation sent a group of its prominent composers, which included Shostakovich and Dmitry Kabalevsky. In its second tour, the United States wanted to send Aaron Copland and Elliott Carter. However, Carter declined this invitation,[227] citing his disapproval of the lack of support American composers were receiving from the US government in comparison to the Soviet government's support of theirs. More specifically, Carter was dissatisfied with the performance opportunities that American composers' (i.e., his own) new works were afforded in their own country and did not see any personal benefit to the prospect of the US now granting performance to the Soviet composers instead. As Carter explained not-so-diplomatically in his response to Frederick Cowell, Chief of the State Department's American Specialist Branch of the International Educational Exchange Program, "the leading Soviet composers have been played more widely in the United States than any American composers." Further, Carter continued voicing his own frustration by noting that "no US performers or orchestras have ever played any work of mine on their trips to the Soviet Union," before adding that "the Soviet orchestras visiting the US play Soviet music here, and when American composers go to Russia a lot more Soviet music is played for them there."[228]

Carter's resentment toward the Soviet composers' opportunities leads us to assume that Carter was unaware of the political conditions and restrictions under which they were living and composing. This notion was further supported by Carter's reversal of his views by 1967 when he gave a series of talks at the Sarah Lawrence College about the oppression and censorship of the Soviet composers ahead of a concert dedicated to avant-garde Soviet music.[229] By this time, Carter must have been fully aware of the circumstances of his privilege and also why specifically his music, with all its extreme complexities and his

---

[225] Meyer and Shreffler, *Elliott Carter: A Centennial Portrait in Letters and Documents*, 159.

[226] Quoted in Meyer and Shreffler, *Elliott Carter: A Centennial Portrait in Letters and Documents*, 159. Also see [Ansari], *"Aaron Copland Meets Soviet Composers: A Television Special,"* 379–92, esp. 380.

[227] Lukas Foss took Carter's place on the Soviet tour of 1960 with Copland.

[228] Elliott Carter to Frederick A. Colwell, January 28, 1960, Correspondence, Elliott Carter Collection (Paul Sacher Stiftung). The complete correspondence between Carter and Colwell is published in Meyer and Shreffler, *Elliott Carter: A Centennial Portrait in Letters and Documents*, 160–61. Nicolas Slonimsky similarly noted after his trip to the Soviet Union in 1970 that "countries are offended when less advanced composers, such as Barber and Copland, are offered to them"; quoted in Fosler-Lussier, *Music in America's Cold War Diplomacy*, 24.

[229] The recordings of these lectures are housed at the Paul Sacher Stiftung. The lectures were published as an edited essay in Carter, "Soviet Music." Also, see Guberman, "Composing Freedom," 194–200.

freedom to explore new ideas, was a perfect counter to the Soviet government-controlled, moderated, and censored works. Carter further embraced this notion of American cultural freedom by adopting concepts such as "new virtuosity," whose development the scholars have attributed to his music, pioneered in String Quartet No. 1.[230]

Whether or not Carter was a knowing participant in the US government's ploy to promote its anticommunist message during the Cold War, it cannot be disputed that he was an extraordinary and exemplary beneficiary. Nonetheless, understanding the context of Carter's participation in the cultural Cold War, under the wing of Nicolas Nabokov, the Congress for Cultural Freedom, the US State Department, and the CIA, explains Carter's newly found success in Europe (and subsequently in the US) with his String Quartet No. 1. As Taruskin surmises, by playing a central role in the cultural Cold War, Carter was insulated from negative critique, rewarded with every prize, enjoyed a major career, and achieved true historical significance.[231] This narrative alone tells us how powerful was the machinery that supported him and stood by him every step of the way. Without the context of Cold War politics, it is virtually impossible to imagine that Carter's String Quartet No. 1 would have achieved such triumph during any other epoch; it was a piece that was needed, specifically at the time it was created. That is, in the early 1950s, Carter's String Quartet No. 1 portrayed American values and artistic freedoms in a most exemplary way. As Martin Boykan effectively remarks, the quartet "spoke ... for the America in the Fifties, in the same way that the Sacre spoke for the Europe of a half-century ago."[232]

Epilogue: The Paved Road to Success

At the 2011 Society for Music Theory meeting in Minneapolis, Elizabeth Hellmuth Margulis presented a talk on the topic of "Empirical Approaches to Repetition in Music."[233] Unbeknownst to the audience members – a roomful of "PhD-holding music theorists" – she conducted an experiment on repetition in "challenging contemporary art music"; more specifically, the musical examples featured pieces by Luciano Berio and Elliott Carter.[234] What also the participants of the experiment did not know is that Margulis had manipulated the one-minute

---

[230] For instance, see Carter's lectures from 1967, "Toward 'New Virtuosity'" and "Toward Metric Virtuosity" in Emmery, *Elliott Carter Speaks*, 52–59.

[231] Taruskin, *The Oxford History of Western Music*, vol. 5, 280.

[232] Boykan, "Elliott Carter and the Postwar Composers," 125.

[233] Margulis, "Empirical Approaches to Repetition in Music." The study was published in Margulis, "Aesthetic Responses to Repetition in Unfamiliar Music."

[234] Margulis, *On Repeat: How Music Plays the Mind*, 15.

musical excerpts by extracting and reinserting segments of music to add repetition of some material. Repetitions were generated randomly by a computer and could occur immediately or after a delay. Without letting the audience know, the adapted versions created by "brute stimulus manipulation without regard to artistic quality" were mixed in with the original works by Berio and Carter, that is, the versions "crafted by internationally renowned composers."[235]

Margulis conducted the same experiment with nonspecialists in 2012. The results are fascinating: she concluded that the listeners preferred the adapted versions of these works over the original. That is, the nonexpert listeners rated the manipulated version with inserted repetitions "as reliably more enjoyable, more interesting, and more likely to have been composed by a human artist rather than generated randomly by a computer," while the SMT audience, comprising experts and scholars of twentieth-century music, or as Margulis puts it, "an audience sympathetic to Berio and Carter if ever there were one," admitted that the repetitive versions were "more likable on first pass."[236] For Margulis, the notion that inserting simple repetition in music could raise the listener's positive experience of music was stunning. However, what I find even more striking in this experiment is that no one in the SMT audience, comprising expert scholars of Elliott Carter's music, knew that the music by Carter that they were listening to had been changed.

Margulis's experiment, which took place after the 2008 centenary events celebrating Carter's music, confirms that even after seven decades of scholarship, concerts, and recordings we really don't know Carter's music. This begs the question: How well did anyone know Carter's String Quartet No. 1 in the 1950s? I would have to conclude not well, and certainly fewer people did than today. But just like today, early critics and scholars (and even the US government) ensured that we know *about* Carter's quartet, even without actually *knowing* it.

From early on, the quartet was painted as the best work of music produced in recent history. In a seventeen-page article dating from 1953, the first article to detail Carter's music and techniques, Abraham Skulsky, a Belgian composer and critic, proclaimed the quartet "a unique work," before continuing that "it may be said to be not only Carter's highest achievement to date but also one of the best works in this form to have appeared during recent years."[237] However, despite these early efforts that highlighted Carter's quartet and his new techniques in the most compelling terms, the audiences, performers, and some critics struggled to understand or even appreciate Carter's quartet, let alone like it. Carter's quartet

---

[235] Margulis, *On Repeat: How Music Plays the Mind*, 15–16.

[236] Margulis, *On Repeat: How Music Plays the Mind*, 15–16.

[237] Skulsky, "Elliott Carter," 10.

was undeniably too complex to understand, too challenging to listen to, and too difficult to perform. Margulis explains that she specifically chose the excerpts by Carter for her experiment for these reasons: they are "atonal, rhythmically complex, and challenging, yet many committed and sophisticated listeners find them deeply rewarding aesthetically."[238] Yet, all participants found the aurally "simplified" version of the piece – a computer-generated adaptation with inserted receptions – more aesthetically rewarding. That is, for most listeners, Carter's music (including his String Quartet No. 1) is impenetrable. Early critics tended to downplay this exigent trait. For instance, Tere Pascone noted in his 1953 review: "But despite the fact that his music is considered difficult to perform and that only few serious-minded performers have been willing to play them, they have met with much success, judging from newspaper and magazine reviews."[239]

Carter Harmon in his *New York Times* review downright dismissed the need for enjoyment of Carter's music, as the experience of listening to it is its own strength: "One of the C's (Copland, Carter, Cowell) whose star is rising is Elliott Carter. Mr. Carter is not a derivative composer. His music seems not only entirely his own, but also uncompromisingly hewn from fresh timber. It gives little sensuous pleasure, but always speaks with strength and leaves the listener with the sense of an important experience."[240]

Skulsky praised the work, emphasizing its "different speeds" that resulted in "a new dimension of music" and that the quartet featured "a unique expressive quality" that created "a large array of different human feelings in a profound, logical and novel organization of ideas."[241] Similarly to Pascone, Skulsky also tried to justify the difficulty of the performance of the work in the context of its success: "In almost every case in recent years, his works have had considerable success as can be seen in the reviews printed elsewhere in this issue. Indeed in learning his works the performers have generally become enthusiastic about them and have played them frequently wherever they could."[242]

Of course, this is not entirely true. For one, Carter himself acknowledged that the performers tend to "grumble about" the difficulty of his music. When Jonathan Bernard asked Carter in a 1990 interview if he thinks that his music is easier to play now than it had been in the past, Carter responded by revealing that the Arditti Quartet had a hard time with his String Quartet No. 5, which they still found to be the most difficult one to play.[243] Allan Kozinn also confirmed

---

238 Margulis, "Aesthetic Responses to Repetition in Unfamiliar Music," 49.
239 Pascone, "Four Honors Fall to Elliott Carter, Southporters' Son."
240 Quoted in Skulsky, "Elliott Carter," 11.
241 Skulsky, "Elliott Carter," 10.
242 Skulsky, "Elliott Carter," 10.
243 Bernard and Carter, "An Interview with Elliott Carter," 184.

this challenge nearly two decades later. In his review of the 2008 Carter Centenary celebration at Tanglewood, the critic first revealed James Levine's plan to "transform the Boston Symphony Orchestra into a first-rate Carter ensemble, with all the composer's major works in the repertory," and then swiftly noted the orchestra's reaction to this plan: "The word is that the orchestra grumbles about its new-music load."[244] This hardly conveys the attitude of enthusiasm in performing Carter's music, even decades later.

From the start, Carter's music was criticized for being too difficult, a notion that would follow him for the rest of his life. This is precisely why Carter and his early supporters found it necessary to contextualize his String Quartet No. 1 within the European tradition of Schoenberg, Berg, Bartók, and Stravinsky, even if that meant acknowledging those influences and the assimilation of their styles in Carter's music before recognizing his unique expression. For instance, Arthur Berger noted in 1953: "Carter is writing some of the most adult and substantial music that is being written anywhere nowadays. He achieves weight without grandiosity. His mind has been alert to all that is worthwhile in tradition, and he has created an original and impressive idiom out of sources as widely dissimilar as Copland, Stravinsky and Schoenberg."[245]

In the context of the Cold War, especially with the formation of the Congress for Cultural Freedom and following Carter's success in Liège and Rome, critics started to downplay or entirely exclude discussing Carter's quartet in the context of its European tradition. Instead, they shifted the focus to Carter's authentic American sound, even though there was hardly anything truly "American" in his quartet. This sense of nationalism and Carter's "Americanness" is effectively conveyed in a letter Wolf wrote to Carter upon learning that an American had won the competition in Liège:

> In utmost seriousness let me say that your quartet provided me with one of the few truly moving musical experiences I have had since coming to Europe a year ago. From its first bars I said "American"; it was a language, musical and personal, that "signified" for me, that communicated in a way that little I have heard here has done. Whatever divergences of specific technique exist between your compositional vocabulary and mine, the essence remains in common, and I am deeply grateful for the communication (which has probably paralyzed me creatively for another three weeks!). Living among Europeans who read the daily papers one has so few occasions to be proud of being American, a matter of small importance in itself but one which does blunt the daily attacks of my student friends. Thanks![246]

---

244 Kozinn, "A Century Has Passed; His Time Is Still Now."
245 Berger, "Music: Composers," 17.
246 Robert Erich Wolf to Elliott Carter, October 9, 1953, Elliott Carter Collection, Correspondence (Paul Sacher Stiftung); quoted in Guberman, "Composing Freedom," 158.

Yet, Wolf's 1957 review of the quartet makes no mention of Carter's "Americanness" in his discussion of the work's musical language but rather focuses on the composer's rhythmic, harmonic, and formal techniques, which are grounded on European traditions. After all, it would be rather difficult to talk about American sound in a piece that does not have any such characteristic traits. That is, the only time Carter had any "Americanness" in his music was during his neoclassical, populist period of the 1930s and 40s, which after the Second World War came to be associated with Socialist Realism in the Soviet Union, a concept from which Carter sought to distance himself with his String Quartet No. 1. Anne Shreffler rightly observes that especially when compared to the "'typically American' experimental tradition of Cage and Feldman, Carter seems to have more in common with his European contemporaries like Boulez."[247] Even Boulez himself thought of Carter as a more European than American composer in his discussion with Marc Ponthus:

> Among the American composers, [Carter's] certainly the most European cultivated. He has more European culture than American. His only truly American moment was Pocahontas, at this period (c. 1939), all American composers tried to be genuinely "American." I organized a mini festival focused on the works of Charles Ives when I was with the New York Philharmonic. It was a study of the evolution of the arts, not only in music but also painting during the 20's and 30's, especially during the Great Depression. During this time, this evolution was parallel to what happened in the Soviet Union, there was a need to be populist, culture had to be accessible to everyone. There was also a change in Russia and there was very strong political pressure in the Soviet Union but in America that was under a kind of New Deal depression expression! An example is Aaron Copland, who wrote Piano Variations and the Short Symphony, which were very much under the influence of Stravinsky, and then suddenly wrote music that was folk music that suppose [sic] to make people dance and be very cheerful. This period corresponded to the paintings found in Mexico during the same period. That was the only period when Elliott Carter had a moment of populist culture in his output. After the war, it was very different. It was interesting to read the articles he wrote for [*New Music Quarterly*] ... you could really see his taste changing progressively.[248]

Ironically, like many other composers who eventually came to be recognized for their "Americanness," perhaps most notably Copland, Carter, too, developed his "American sound" in Paris, before abandoning his studies upon his return to the United States. That is, after completing his degree at Harvard in 1932, Carter

---

[247] Shreffler, "Elliott Carter and His America," 39.

[248] Ponthus and Tang, *Elliott Carter: A Centennial Celebration*, 6–7. The conversation took place on April 12, 2007 at the Berlin's Staatsoper.

left New York for Paris to study with Nadia Boulanger and escape his disappointingly conservative education in Boston with Walter Piston. However, by that time, Carter notes, "this whole extravagant world of crazy modernism began to seem a little bit old" to Boulanger.[249] Thus, rather than writing modernist music, Carter honed in on his neoclassical and populist aesthetic during this period, as he explains: "It's only after I studied with Nadia, that there was this whole, sort of, more socialist point of view about everything. We all thought that we should write for a larger public and not write this special music that only special people could understand."[250]

With his String Quartet No. 1, Carter returned to his earlier musical thinking, the ideas his teachers, Walter Piston and Nadia Boulanger, did not approve or encourage, or even like; as he sums up, "They couldn't teach me what I wanted to learn."[251] In post–Second World War America, Carter succeeded in escaping his French-oriented neoclassicism but could not avoid using his traditional European training and techniques. But it was precisely his European sound that made String Quartet No. 1 a big success in Europe and less so in the United States. Even the techniques Carter "debuted" in quartet were not entirely new – he explored instrumental virtuosity in his Piano Sonata (1945–46) and in the Cello Sonata (1948), *Eight Etudes and a Fantasy* (1949–50), and *Eight Pieces for Four Timpani* (1949), he applied the concepts of the individualization of the instruments, polyrhythms, metric modulation, and chordal sonorities as a means of unifying a work. Perhaps, Skulsky summed it up most accurately when he wrote that Carter "devoted about a year to his String Quartet which is a gathering together of all the facets of his creative activity so far."[252] So, not quite a "rebirth" or a "conversion" during his not-so "monastic seclusion" in the Sonoran Desert.

What String Quartet No. 1 truly displayed was an effective statement Carter made on distancing himself from the influence of (Nadia Boulanger's) populism, which was crucial in the context of the Cold War. In fact, upon his return to the United States in 1935, Carter composed prolifically in the neoclassical style, including two string quartets that predate *the* "first" Quartet of 1951. Although Carter intentionally destroyed most of these early works, one such piece, the String Quartet in C from 1937, survives in ink fair copy.[253] However, Carter never truly admitted that the work – found among his

---

[249] Emmery, "An American Modernist," 28.

[250] Emmery, "An American Modernist," 28.

[251] Holliger, "Abseits des Mainstreams: Ein Gespräch mit dem Amerikanischen Komponisten Elliott Carter," 8; quoted in Shreffler, "Elliott Carter and His America," 41.

[252] Skulsky, "Elliott Carter," 10.

[253] The other string quartet was written in 1935 and does not survive. See Meyer and Shreffler, *Elliott Carter: A Centennial Portrait in Letters and Documents*, 36–37.

documents, bearing his handwriting, and written in his characteristic style of this period – was attributed to him. Simply, writing a string quartet in C major under the tutelage of Nadia Boulanger did not fit the compelling narrative of the foremost modernist American composer. However, a piece born in the American Southwest, featuring tremendous complexities yet a total disregard for the audiences and performers in the composer's selfish quest to satisfy his own artistic needs, was ideologically as American as it can get in the early years of the Cold War. This political context is exactly what made Carter one of the most recognizable American composers both at home and in Europe. To achieve this status and prestige, with a piece whose content did not have any distinctly "American" originality in it, Carter, with the help of his powerful friends, forged narratives of mythical proportions surrounding the quartet, starting with the desert myth, which Shreffler perfectly describes as "a gesture out of the oldest of American mythologies."[254] The strategy was a success: it is these carefully crafted narratives that have shaped the success, reception, and legacy of Carter and his String Quartet No. 1 that we know and continue to perpetuate.

Ironically (and quite naively), Skulsky concludes that "recognition has come to Carter slowly and without his having made any particular effort to seek it out."[255] As illustrated in this Element, it was the incredibly complex and powerful machinery that contributed to Carter's accomplishment of his String Quartet No. 1. The truly surprising outcome would have been if Carter had not succeeded, for his triumph was meticulously paved.

---

[254] Shreffler, "Elliott Carter and His America," 40.
[255] Skulsky, "Elliott Carter," 11.

Bibliography

Archival Sources

Elliott Carter Collection. Sketches for String Quartet No. 1 (1951). Library of Congress, Washington, DC. http://lcweb2.loc.gov/diglib/ihas/loc.natlib .ihas.200155638/default.html.

Elliott Carter Papers, 1945–95 [bulk 1980–95]. New York Public Library Archives and Manuscripts.

The Elliott Carter Collection. Correspondence. Paul Sacher Stiftung, Basel, Switzerland.

Sketches for String Quartet No. 1 (1950–51). Paul Sacher Stiftung, Basel, Switzerland.

String Quartet No. 1, "Einführungstext" [Introduction]. Paul Sacher Stiftung, Basel, Switzerland.

"Time Lecture." Paul Sacher Stiftung, Basel, Switzerland.

Published Sources

Adlington, Robert. 2020. "Curating Difference: Elliott Carter and Democracy." In *Finding Democracy in Music*, ed. Robert Adlington and Esteban Buch, 80–100. London: Routledge.

Altizer, Thomas J. J. 1997. *The Self-Embodiment of God*. San Francisco: Harper and Row.

d'Amico, Fedele. 1954. "Current Chronicle." *The Musical Quarterly* 40 (4): 587–94.

[Ansari] Abrams, Emily. 2005. "*Aaron Copland Meets Soviet Composers*: A Television Special," transcribed and introduced by Emily Abrams. In *Aaron Copland and His World*, ed. Carol J. Oja and Judith Tick, 379–92. Princeton: Princeton University Press.

2011. "Aaron Copland and the Politics of Cultural Diplomacy." *Journal of the Society for American Music* 5 (3): 335–64.

Barnhisel, Greg. 2015. *Cold War Modernists: Art, Literature, and American Cultural Diplomacy*. New York: Columbia University Press.

Berger, Arthur. 1953. "Music: Composers." *Saturday Review*, March 14: 17–18.

Bernard, Jonathan W. 1988. "The Evolution of Elliott Carter's Rhythmic Practice." *Perspectives of New Music* 26 (2): 164–203.

1993. "Problems of Pitch Structure in Elliott Carter's First and Second String Quartets." *Journal of Music Theory* 37 (2): 231–66.

1995. "Elliott Carter and the Modern Meaning of Time." *The Musical Quarterly* 79 (4): 644–82.

2009. "The String Quartets of Elliott Carter." In *Intimate Voices: The Twentieth-Century String Quartet*, vol. 2, ed. Evan Jones, 238–75. Rochester: University of Rochester Press.

Bernard, Jonathan W., and Elliott Carter. 1990. "An Interview with Elliott Carter." *Perspectives of New Music* 28 (2): 180–214.

Bose, Sudip. 2018. "A Year in the Desert: Elliott Carter and His Revolutionary First String Quartet." *The American Scholar*, January 11. https://theamer icanscholar.org/a-year-in-the-desert/.

Boykan, Martin. 1964. "Elliott Carter and the Postwar Composers." *Perspectives of New Music* 2 (2): 125–28.

Brindle, Reginald Smith. 1954. "Notes from Abroad." *The Musical Times* 95 (1336): 328–29.

Brody, Martin. 2014a. "Class of '54: Friendship and Ideology at the American Academy in Rome." In *Music and Musical Composition at the American Academy in Rome*, ed. Martin Brody, 222–54. Rochester: University of Rochester Press.

2014b. "Cold War Genius: Music and Cultural Diplomacy at the American Academy in Rome." In *Crosscurrents: American and European Music in Interaction, 1900–2000*, ed. Felix Meyer, Carol J. Oja, Wolfgang Rathert, and Anne Shreffler, 375–87. Woodbridge: Boydell & Brewer.

Bruhn, Siglind. 1997. *Images and Ideas in Modern French Piano Music: The Extra-Musical Subtext in Piano Works by Ravel, Debussy, and Messiaen.* Stuyvesant: Pendragon Press.

2000. *Musical Ekphrasis: Composers Responding to Poetry and Painting.* Hillsdale: Pendragon Press.

Carr, Maureen A. 2014. *After the Rite: Stravinsky's Path to Neoclassicism (1914–1925).* Oxford: Oxford University Press.

Carter, Elliott. 1960. "Shop Talk by an American Composer." *The Musical Quarterly* 46 (2): 189–201.

1997 (1939). "The Case of Mr. Ives." In *Elliott Carter: Collected Essays and Lectures, 1937–1997*, ed. Jonathan W. Bernard, 87–90. Rochester: University of Rochester Press.

1997 (1944). "Ives Today: His Vision and Challenge." In *Elliott Carter: Collected Essays and Lectures, 1937–1997*, ed. Jonathan W. Bernard, 90–93. Rochester: University of Rochester Press.

1997 (1946). "An American Destiny." In *Elliott Carter: Collected Essays and Lectures, 1937–1997*, ed. Jonathan W. Bernard, 93–98. Rochester: University of Rochester Press.

1997 (1955). "The Rhythmic Basis of American Music." In *Elliott Carter: Collected Essays and Lectures, 1937–1997*, ed. Jonathan W. Bernard, 57–62. Rochester: University of Rochester Press.

1997 (1963). "Letter from Europe." In *Elliott Carter: Collected Essays and Lectures, 1937–1997*, ed. Jonathan W. Bernard, 31–40. Rochester: University of Rochester Press.

1997 (1965/94). "La Musique sérielle aujourd'hui." In *Elliott Carter: Collected Essays and Lectures, 1937–1997*, ed. Jonathan W. Bernard, 17–18. Rochester: University of Rochester Press.

1997 (1967/94). "Soviet Music." In *Elliott Carter: Collected Essays and Lectures, 1937–1997*, ed. Jonathan W. Bernard, 331–35. Rochester: University of Rochester Press.

1997 (1970). "String Quartets Nos. 1, 1951, and 2, 1959." In *Elliott Carter: Collected Essays and Lectures, 1937–1997*, ed. Jonathan W. Bernard, 231–35. Rochester: University of Rochester Press.

1997 (1974). "Charles Ives Remembered." In *Elliott Carter: Collected Essays and Lectures, 1937–1997*, ed. Jonathan W. Bernard, 98–107. Rochester: University of Rochester Press.

1997 (1975). "Documents of a Friendship with Ives." In *Elliott Carter: Collected Essays and Lectures, 1937–1997*, ed. Jonathan W. Bernard, 107–18. Rochester: University of Rochester Press.

1997 (1976). "Music and the Time Screen." In *Elliott Carter: Collected Essays and Lectures, 1937–1997*, ed. Jonathan W. Bernard, 262–80. Rochester: University of Rochester Press.

Carter, Elliott, and Benjamin Boretz. 1970. "Conversation with Elliott Carter." *Perspectives of New Music* 8 (2): 1–22.

Chou, Wen-Chung. 1966. "Varèse: A Sketch of the Man and His Music." *The Musical Quarterly* 52 (2): 161–70.

Cocteau, Jean, dir. 1930. *Le Sang d'un poète*. The Criterion Collection.

Copland, Aaron, and Vivian Perlis. 1984. *Copland: 1900 through 1942*. New York: St. Martin's Press.

Coroniti, Jr., Joseph A. 1989. "Scoring the 'Absolute Rhythm' of Williams Carlos Williams: Steve Reich's 'The Desert Music.'" *William Carlos Williams Review* 15 (2): 36–48.

Coulembier, Klaas. 2012. "Elliott Carter's Structural Polyrhythms in the 1970s: 'A Mirror on Which to Dwell.'" *Tempo* 66 (261): 12–25.

Crane, Hart. 1930. *The Bridge*. Paris: Black Sun Press.

Edwards, Allen. 1972. *Flawed Words and Stubborn Sounds: A Conversation with Elliott Carter*. New York: W. W. Norton & Co.

Eliot, T. S. 1922. *The Waste Land*. New York: Boni & Liveright.

Emmery, Laura. 2013a. "An American Modernist: Teatime with Elliott Carter." *Tempo* 67 (264): 22–29.

———. 2013b. "Rhythmic Process in Elliott Carter's Fourth String Quartet." *Mitteilungen der Paul Sacher Stiftung* 26: 34–38.

———. 2014. "Evolution and Process in Elliott Carter's String Quartets." Ph.D. diss., University of California, Santa Barbara.

———. 2015. "In Disguise: Musical Borrowings in Elliott Carter's Early String Quartets." In *Form and Process in Music, 1300–2014: An Analytical Sampler*, ed. Jack Boss, Heather Holmquest, Russell Knight, Inés Thiebaut, and Brent Yorgason, 125–46. Newcastle: Cambridge Scholars Publishing.

———. 2019. "Elliott Carter's First String Quartet: In Search of Proustian Time." *The Musical Quarterly* 102 (4): 440–80.

———. 2020. *Compositional Process in Elliott Carter's String Quartets: A Study in Sketches*. New York: Routledge.

———. 2022. *Elliott Carter Speaks: Unpublished Lectures*. Urbana: University of Illinois Press.

Feldman, Morton. 2000 (1971). "Give My Regards to Eighth Street (1971)." In *Give My Regards to Eighth Street: Collected Writings of Morton Feldman*, ed. B. H. Friedman, 93–101. Cambridge, MA: Exact Change.

Fiechtner, Helmuth A. 1954. "Tonkunst und Debatten beim Römischen Musikkongreß." *Österreichische Musikzeitschrift* 9 (5): 159–60.

Fosler-Lussier, Danielle. 2015. *Music in America's Cold War Diplomacy*. Oakland: University of California Press.

Frankel, Max. 1967. "Ex-Official of C.I.A. Lists Big Grants to Labor Aides." *New York Times*, May 8, 1967: 1, 36. https://timesmachine.nytimes.com/timesmachine/1967/05/08/issue.html.

Frankenstein, Alfred. 1956. "California String Quartet Offers Concert Eloquence." *San Francisco Chronicle*, January 5, 1956: 25.

Fox, Sylvan. 1967. "Stephen Spender Quits Encounter: British Poet Says Finding of C.I.A. Financing Led to His Leaving Magazine." *New York Times*, May 8, 1967: 1, 37. https://timesmachine.nytimes.com/timesmachine/1967/05/08/issue.html.

Gillespie, Don. 2009. "Chou Wen-Chung on Varèse: An Interview." *American Music* 27 (4): 441–60.

Goehr, Lydia. 2010. "How to Do More with Words: Two Views of (Musical) Ekphrasis." *The British Journal of Aesthetics* 50 (4): 389–410.

Goldman, Richard Franko. 1957. "The Music of Elliott Carter." *The Musical Quarterly* 43 (2): 151–70.

Guberman, Daniel. 2012. "Composing Freedom: Elliott Carter's 'Self-Reinvention' and the Early Cold War." Ph.D. diss., University of North Carolina at Chapel Hill.

———. 2021. "Victory in Liège? Elliott Carter and the Diplomacy of International Competitions." *Elliott Carter Studies Online* 4. https://studies.elliottcarter .org/volume04/01Guberman/01Guberman.html.

Harris, Sarah Miller. 2016. *The CIA and the Congress for Cultural Freedom in the Early Cold War: The Limits of Making Common Sense*. New York: Routledge.

Hilewicz, Orit. 2018. "Reciprocal Interpretations of Music and Painting: Representation Types in Schuller, Tan, and Davies after Paul Klee." *Music Theory Online* 24 (3). https://mtosmt.org/issues/mto.18.24.3/ mto.18.24.3.hilewicz.html.

Holliger, Heinz. 1991. "Abseits des Mainstreams: Ein Gespräch mit dem Amerikanischen Komponisten Elliott Carter." *Neue Zeitschrift für Musik* 152 (3): 4–9.

Iber, Patrick. 2015. *Neither Peace nor Freedom: The Cultural Cold War in Latin America*. Cambridge, MA: Harvard University Press.

———. 2017. "The Spy Who Funded Me: Revisiting the Congress for Cultural Freedom." *Los Angeles Review of Books*, June 11, 2017. https://lareviewof books.org/article/the-spy-who-funded-me-revisiting-the-congress-for-cul tural-freedom/.

Jasper, David. 2004. *The Sacred Desert: Religion, Literature, Art, and Culture*. Oxford: Blackwell Publishing.

Jenkins, J. Daniel. 2010. "After the Harvest: Carter's Fifth String Quartet and the Late Late Style." *Music Theory Online* 16 (3).

Kerman, Joseph. 1958. "American Music: The Columbia Series." *The Hudson Review* 11 (3): 420–30.

Klemm, David E. 2004. "Foreword." In *The Sacred Desert: Religion, Literature, Art, and Culture*, David Jasper, xi–xiv. Oxford: Blackwell Publishing.

Koch, Martine. 2019. *Louis Poulet & le concours international de quatuor à cordes de la ville de Liège: Composition–interpretation–lutherie (1951–1972)*, illustrated ed. Liège: Les éditions de la province de Liège.

Kozinn, Allan. 2008. "A Century Has Passed; His Time Is Still Now." *New York Times*, July 26, 2008. www.nytimes.com/2008/07/26/arts/music/26cont .html.

Krutch, Joseph Wood. 1952. *The Desert Year*. New York: The Viking Press.

Levy, Beth E. 2012. *Frontier Figures: American Music and the Mythology of the American West*. Berkeley: University of California Press.

Link, John F. 1994. "Long-range Polyrhythms in Elliott Carter's Recent Music." Ph.D. diss., University of New York.

Lochhead, Judy. 1994. "On the 'Framing' Music of Elliott Carter's First String Quartet." In *Musical Transformation and Musical Intuition: Eleven Essays in Honor of David Lewin*, ed. Raphael Atlas and Michael Cherlin, 179–98. Roxbury: Ovenbird Press.

Lowney, John. 2004. "Reading the Borders of 'The Desert Music.'" *William Carlos Williams Review* 24 (2): 61–77.

Mailman, Joshua B. 2010. "Temporal Dynamic Form in Music: Atonal, Tonal, and Other." Ph.D. diss., University of Rochester.

Margulis, Elizabeth Hellmuth. 2011. "Empirical Approaches to Repetition in Music." Paper presented at the Society for Music Theory, October 29, 2011, Minneapolis.

　　2013. "Aesthetic Responses to Repetition in Unfamiliar Music." *Empirical Studies of the Arts* 31 (1): 45–57.

　　2014. *On Repeat: How Music Plays the Mind*. New York: Oxford University Press.

Mattis, Olivia. 1992. "Varèse's Multimedia Conception of 'Déserts.'" *The Musical Quarterly* 76 (4): 557–83.

Mead, Andrew 2012. "Time Management: Rhythm as a Formal Determinant in Certain Works of Elliott Carter." In *Elliott Carter Studies*, ed. Marguerite Boland and John Link, 138–67. Cambridge, UK: Cambridge University Press.

Mead, Rita H. 1981. *Henry Cowell's New Music, 1925–1936: The Society, the Music Editions, and the Recordings*. Ann Arbor: UMI Research Press.

Meyer, Felix, and Anne C. Shreffler. 2008. *Elliott Carter: A Centennial Portrait in Letters and Documents*. Suffolk: The Boydell Press.

Myers, Neil. 1970. "Williams' Imitation of Nature in "The Desert Music." *Criticism* 12 (1): 38–50.

The Nation Editorial. 1964. "Foundations as 'Fronts.'" *The Nation*, September 14, 1964: 102–3.

Noubel, Max. 2000. *Elliott Carter ou le temps fertile*. Geneva: Éditions Contrechamps.

Office of the Historian. n.d. "Marshall Plan, 1948." The United States of America, Department of State. https://history.state.gov/milestones/1945-1952/marshall-plan.

Oja, Carol J. 2000. *Making Music Modern: New York in the 1920s*. New York: Oxford University Press.

Pascone, Tere. 1953. "Four Honors Fall to Elliott Carter, Southporters' Son." *The Bridgepost Sunday.* Accessed via the New York Public Library, Elliott Carter Papers archive.

Perse, Saint-John. 1961. *Winds*, bilingual ed., trans. Hugh Chisholm. New York: Pantheon Books.

Ponthus, Marc, and Susan Tang, eds. 2008. *Elliott Carter: A Centennial Celebration.* Festschrift Series 23. Hillsdale, NY: Pendragon Press.

Poudrier, Ève. 2008. "Toward a General Theory of Polymeter: Polymetric Potential and Realization in Elliott Carter's Solo and Chamber Instrumental Works after 1980." Ph.D. diss., City University of New York.

Proust, Marcel. 1981–82 (1913–27). *Remembrance of Things Past, Vol. 1: Swann's Way & Within a Budding Grove*, trans. C. K. Scott Moncrieff and T. Kilmartin. New York: Random House, 1981. Vol. 2: *The Guermantes Way & Cities of the Plain*, trans. C. K. Scott Moncrieff and T. Kilmartin. New York: Random House, 1982. Vol. 3: *The Captive, The Fugitive & Time Regained*, trans. C. K. Scott Moncrieff, T. Kilmartin, and Andreas Mayor. New York: Random House, 1982.

Rao, Nancy Yunhwa. 2014. "*Allegro scorrevole* in Carter's Frist String Quartet: Crawford and the Ultramodern Inheritance." *Music Theory Spectrum* 36 (2): 181–202.

Rochberg, George. 1957. "Review, Elliott Carter: Quartet by Elliott Carter." *The Musical Quarterly* 43 (1): 130–32.

Rosen, Charles. 2011. "Music and the Cold War." *The New York Review of Books* April 7, 2011. www.nybooks.com/articles/2011/04/07/music-and-cold-war/?pagination=false&printpage=true.

Said, Edward W. 2001. "A Standing Civil War." In *Reflections on Exile and Other Literary and Cultural Essays*, 31–40. London: Granta Books.

Salzedo, Carlos. 2026. "Outward Shows." *Eolus* 5 (2), May 1926.

Saunders, Frances Stonor. 1999. "How the CIA Plotted against Us." *New Statesman*, July 12, 1999. Last access July 8, 2024. https://web.archive.org/web/20141010045414/http://www.newstatesman.com/node/135185.

    2000 (1999). *Who Paid the Piper? The Cultural Cold War: The CIA and the World of Arts and Letters.* London: Granta Books.

Schiff, David. 1998 (1983). *The Music of Elliott Carter*, 2nd ed. London: Faber and Faber.

    2018. *Carter.* New York: Oxford University Press.

Schmidt, Dörte. 2012. "'I Try to Write Music that Will Appeal to an Intelligent Listener's Ear.' On Elliott Carter's String Quartets." In *Elliott Carter Studies*, ed. Marguerite Boland and John Link, 168–89. Cambridge, UK: Cambridge University Press.

Schoenberg, Arnold. 1950. "Brahms the Progressive (1947)." In *Style and Idea*, 52–101, New York: Philosophical Library, Inc.

1960. "The Orchestral Variations, Op. 31: A Radio Talk." *The Score* 27: 27–40.

1975. "Composition with Twelve Tones (1) (1941)." In *Style and Idea: Selected Writings of Arnold Schoenberg*, ed. Leonard Stein, trans. Leo Black, 214–45. London: Faber and Faber Limited.

1975. "Schoenberg's Tone-Rows (1936)." In *Style and Idea: Selected Writings of Arnold Schoenberg*, ed. Leonard Stein, trans. Leo Black, 213–14. London: Faber and Faber Limited.

Scott-Smith, Giles. 2002. *The Politics of Apolitical Culture: The Congress for Cultural Freedom and the Political Economy of American Hegemony 1945–1955*. London: Routledge.

Sheehan, Neil. 1967. "A Student Group Concedes It Took Funds from C.I.A." *New York Times*, February 14, 1967.

Shreffler, Anne C. 1994. "Elliott Carter and His America." *Sonus* 14 (2): 38–66.

2000. "The Myth of Empirical Historiography: A Response to Joseph N. Straus." *The Musical Quarterly* 84 (1): 30–39.

Skulsky, Abraham. 1953. "Elliott Carter." *Bulletin of American Composers Alliance* 3 (2): 2–11.

Souriau, Étienne. 1966. *La poésie française et la peinture*. London: Athlone Press.

Steinberg, Michael. 1954. "Rome Fete Hears 3 Chamber Works." *New York Times*, April 13, 1954: 40.

Straus, Joseph N. 1999. "The Myth of Serial 'Tyranny' in the 1950s and 1960s." *The Musical Quarterly* 83 (3): 301–43.

Taruskin, Richard. 2005. *The Oxford History of Western Music*, vol. 5: The Late Twentieth Century. Oxford: Oxford University Press.

2009. "Afterword: Nicht blutbefleckt?" *The Journal of Musicology* 26 (2): 274–84.

Thomson, Virgil. 2014. *Music Chronicles, 1940–1954*. New York: The Library of America.

Thoreau, Henry David. 1893. "Walking." In *Excursions: The Writings of Henry David Thoreau*, Riverside ed., 11 vols., vol. 9, 251–304. Boston: Houghton Miflin Company.

Tynan, Aidan. 2020. *The Desert in Modern Literature and Philosophy: Wasteland Aesthetics*. Edinburgh: Edinburgh University Press.

de Vries, Tity. 2012. "The 1967 Central Intelligence Agency Scandal: Catalyst in a Transforming Relationship between State and People." *The Journal of American History* 98 (4): 1075–92.

Wellens, Ian. 2016 (2002). *Music on the Frontline: Nicolas Nabokov's Struggle against Communism and Middlebrow Culture*. London and New York: Routledge.

Whitney, Joel. 2017. *Finks: How the C.I.A. Tricked the World's Best Writers*. New York: OR Books.

Wierzbicki, James. 2011. *Elliott Carter*. Urbana: University of Illinois Press.

Wilford, Hugh. 2008. *The Mighty Wurlitzer: How the CIA Played America*. Cambridge, MA: Harvard University Press.

Williams, William Carlos. 1954. *The Desert Music and Other Poems by William Carlos Williams*. New York: Random House.

Wolf, Robert Erich. 1957. "Review [String Quartet, 1951, by Elliott Carter]." *Notes* 14 (2): 198–99.

Zimmermann, Walter. 1976. *Desert Plants: Conversations with 23 American Musicians*. Vancouver: Walter Zimmermann and A.R.C. Publications.

Zuckerman, Laurence. 2000. "How the C.I.A. Played Dirty Tricks with Culture." *New York Times*, March 18, 2000. www.nytimes.com/2000/03/18/books/how-the-cia-played-dirty-tricks-with-culture.html.

Discography

Carter, Elliott. 1956. *Elliott Carter String Quartet*. The Walden Quartet of the University of Illinois: Homer Schmitt (violin I), Bernard Goodman (violin II), John Garvey (viola), Robert Swenson (cello). Columbia ML 5104.

1970. *Elliott Carter: String Quartets Nos. 1 & 2*. The Composers Quartet: Matthew Raimondi (violin I), Anahid Ajemian (violin II), Jean Dupouy (viola), Michael Rudiakov (cello). Nonesuch H 71249. Reissued on *Elliott Carter: A Nonesuch Retrospective*. Nonesuch 510893-2 (2009). Also issued as Elektra Nonesuch 71249-2 (CD) [after 1983].

1988. *Elliott Carter: The Works for String Quartet, Volume 1: String Quartets 1 & 4*. The Arditti String Quartet: Irvine Arditti (violin I), David Alberman (violin II), Levine Andrade (viola), Rohan De Saram (cello). Etcetera KTC 1065.

1991. *Elliott Carter: The Four String Quartets; Duo for Violin and Piano*. The Juilliard String Quartet: Robert Mann (violin I), Joel Smirnoff (violin II), Samuel Rhodes (viola), Joel Krosnick (cello); Christopher Oldfather (piano). Sony S2K 47229.

2008. *Elliott Carter: String Quartets Nos. 1 & 5*. Pacifica Quartet: Simin Ganatra (violin I), Sibbi Bernhardsson (violin II), Masumi Per Rostad (viola), Brandon Vamos (cello). Naxos 8.559362. Reissued on *Elliott*

Carter: The Complete String Quartets; 100th Anniversary Release. Naxos 8.503225 (2010).

2014. *Elliott Carter: The Five String Quartets*. The Juilliard String Quartet: Robert Mann (violin I), Joel Smirnoff (violin II), Samuel Rhodes (viola), Joel Krosnick (cello). Quartets Nos. 1–4, reissue from *Elliott Carter: The Four String Quartets; Duo for Violin and Piano* (1991). Quartet 5: Joseph Lin (violin I), Ronald Copes (violin II), Samuel Rhodes (viola), Joel Krosnick (cello). Sony 8843-03383-2.

Websites

The Amphion Foundation, Inc. *Elliott Carter.* www.elliottcarter.com/.

The Internet Archive. "Full Text of 'String Quartet.'" https://archive.org/stream/lp_string-quartet_elliott-carter-the-walden-string-quartet/lp_string-quartet_elliott-carter-the-walden-string-quartet_djvu.txt.

Acknowledgments

I would like to thank my family for their continuous support, especially my parents Michael and Maryann.

I would like to express my heartfelt gratitude to Felix Meyer, former director of the Paul Sacher Stiftung (Basel, Switzerland), for sharing his infinite wisdom, knowledge, and insight about the work and life of Elliott Carter. I would like to extend my thanks to the musicologists, archivists, and staff at the Paul Sacher Stiftung for their continuous generosity in providing me with information and granting me publication permissions for this project. Likewise, I am thankful to the *New York Times* and G. Schirmer/Associated Music Publishers for permitting me to publish select documents and score excerpts. I am also grateful to the archivists and staff at the New York Public Library and the Library of Congress in Washington, DC. Further, I would like to thank Peter Shirts, Music Librarian at Emory University, who always goes above and beyond in helping me obtain the necessary materials, of any kind, from anywhere in the world.

I would like to express my enormous gratitude to two anonymous peer reviewers, who put so much thought, care, and professionalism into reading my Element. Your detailed, insightful, and constructive suggestions undoubtedly strengthened and refined my arguments.

Lastly, I am grateful to Mervyn Cooke and the editorial and production team at Cambridge University Press, for believing in this project and for their enthusiasm.

To my beloved brother Robert
May eternal light shine upon you

Music Since 1945

Mervyn Cooke
University of Nottingham

Mervyn Cooke brings to the role of series editor an unusually broad range of expertise, having published widely in the fields of twentieth-century opera, concert and theatre music, jazz, and film music. He has edited and co-edited *Cambridge Companions to Britten, Jazz, Twentieth-Century Opera*, and *Film Music*. His other books include *Britten: War Requiem, Britten and the Far East, A History of Film Music, The Hollywood Film Music Reader, Pat Metheny: The ECM Years*, and two illustrated histories of jazz. He is currently co-editing (with Christopher R. Wilson) *The Oxford Handbook of Shakespeare and Music*.

About the Series

Elements in Music Since 1945 is a highly stimulating collection of authoritative online essays that reflects the latest research into a wide range of musical topics of international significance since the Second World War. Individual Elements are organised into constantly evolving clusters devoted to such topics as art music, jazz, music and image, stage and screen genres, music and media, music and place, immersive music, music and movement, music and politics, music and conflict, and music and society. The latest research questions in theory, criticism, musicology, composition and performance are also given cutting-edge and thought-provoking coverage. The digital-first format allows authors to respond rapidly to new research trends, with contributions being updated to reflect the latest thinking in their fields, and the essays are enhanced by the provision of an exciting range of online resources.

www.ingramcontent.com/pod-product-compliance
Ingram Content Group UK Ltd.
Pitfield, Milton Keynes, MK11 3LW, UK
UKHW022343190125
453804UK00026B/651